Dear Reader,

Victoria Cruises is a US company based in New York which specializes in Yangzi River cruises. In 1994 we began sailing with our first custom designed ship, The Victoria I, and established new standards for service and comfort in Yangzi River cruising. Victoria has now expanded to four sister ships, sailing on a regular schedule downstream between Chongqing and Wuhan for four days, and the reverse upstream itinerary for six days. Our ships were built in China by a shipyard specializing in the manufacture of vessels for the Yangzi. We are responsible for the management of these ships, and all bookings are handled through our New York office.

All our outside suites and cabins have lower berths and a private bathroom. Our standard cabins are 155 square feet with picture windows, affording the perfect opportunity to view the extraordinary views along the Yangzi while relaxing in comfort. Our 160-seat dining room offers excellent Chinese cuisine, as well as Western selections.

The crew of 112 includes English-speaking tour guides and cruise director. Shipboard activities will include a sampling of local Chinese entertainment. A number of facilities are available including a fully-equipped business center, accommodating bar, outdoor jacuzzi, health clinic, beauty salon and reading room.

Among the fascinating sights along the river are the famed Three Gorges, a 193-kilometer stretch of majestic cliffs and spectacular scenery. Shore excursions to ancient towns and remote villages will allow you to see life as it is lived in China's heartland.

Our ships are also available for chartering and itineraries can be adjusted to suit the requirements of a particular group within scheduled sailing dates.

A voyage on the Yangzi is always an unforgettable adventure. We are delighted to offer you this experience in a style and comfort never before available.

Sincerely yours,

James Pi
President

大 江 永 流
The Great River Flows Forever ...

by Richard Perry Hayman, Director of Cruise Operations, Victoria Cruises

I first sailed up the Yangzi River in 1981 on a lumbering, overcrowded transport ship, one of the old 'East is Red' fleet, packed with People's Liberation Army soldiers on leave. Although my bunk cabin was spartan the people were friendly and the journey was exhilarating as I traveled to Chongqing. Here, my grandfather had been advisor to the Nationalist Army during the 1940s; as a boy I was filled with his tales of adventure. Now, as China opened itself to travelers, I had come to see the great River for myself.

Some time later, while working as a cruise director aboard the Kun Lun, the state guest ship built for Chairman Mao, I brought along my folding sailing kayak. One afternoon I took it out for a spin. The crowds on the bank at Zhenjiang greeted me wide-eyed with curiosity. Soon, however, a police launch was speeding along

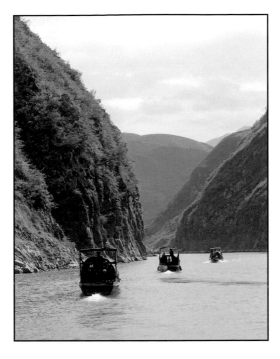

to pluck me and my craft out, claiming that no foreign vessels were allowed on the Yangzi. Although I was flying the UN flag I was still arrested. I was later released to the political commissar aboard the Kun Lun who lectured me for hours in angry Hubeinese.

Now, as I sail in the modern comfort of a new Victoria ship, in a more relaxed and welcoming China, I truly appreciate how much China and the river have changed.

O! The mighty Yangzi! It is a river extolled for centuries, from Li Bai to Marco Polo to Monty Python, and now by many travelers from afar. To the world, the name conjures up visions of the vastness of China, its people living in isolation amidst the countless mountains and waters of inner Asia.

Remarkable in its size and variety, the Yangzi is the only river in the world to have cut across a series of rugged mountain ranges—the spectacular and legendary Three Gorges. It is a geological and mythological wonder. The journey is comparable to a passage on the broad Mississippi through the Grand Canyon with the rich cultural heritage of the Nile. The Yangzi offers more to see and learn than seems humanly possible. This book provides an excellent introduction.

To China, the Yangzi is the heart of the land and the nation. Its name in Chinese is the 'Chang Jiang', the 'Long' or the 'Da Jiang', 'Great River'. Many distinct sections retain traditional names, with innumerable historic and mythical references. The 'Yangzi', with its various spellings, refers to the broad 'ocean' mouth where the far bank is not visible. There,

the first
Europeans
sailed in and
took the local
name to mean
the river's
whole length.

From its
headwaters fed
by glaciers in
Tibet to the
mouth at the
East China Sea,
the Yangzi leaps great rapids, feeds and drains great lakes and
marshes and passes sacred Daoist mountains on its course to
the sea. It has been likened to a great golden dragon, a symbol
for the Middle Kingdom, a source of life in its bounty and a
bearer of miseries in times of flood and famine.

The river gods of old are still said to reside in its
murky waters, even as modernization and industry hold
center stage. Small craft fall victim to the rapids, their
hapless boatmen becoming 'water ghosts'. The launching
of each new ship of the Victoria fleet by the state-owned
shipyard still witnesses the traditional sacrifice of a chick-
en at the bow with popping firecrackers to propitiate the
river spirits—just in case!

The poet Du Fu wrote that 'travelling to Sichuan is more
difficult than climbing to heaven.' Junks laden with goods
bounding up the Yangzi Gorges used to be hauled by hundreds of trackers groaning and singing as they struggled along
paths cut into the cliff face. Later, when steamships made the
same passage, bandits would shoot from the ridges above to

disable the ships before looting them. There is no such trouble today, but the Gorges have been a site of heroic battles and incredible feats from earliest recorded history.

The Yangzi has become a newly appreciated cradle of ancient civilization with the recent discovery of tombs containing exquisite bronze vessels and musical instruments from the Chu Kingdom (338–278 BC). Ba Kingdom artifacts from over 3000 years ago have also been found in the Gorges region. As China has unified, divided and united again, the regions of the Yangzi have maintained their distinct languages and local flavors. Along its banks have passed armies and navies of successive dynasties in the recurrent contest between North and South. The most celebrated battles were

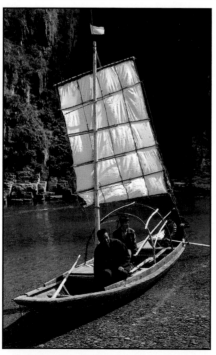

the exploits of the Three Kingdom heroes in the Third Century AD, archetypes of loyalty and strategy to this day. The Chinese classical expression to 'cross the river' refers to a force capable of securing both banks of the Yangzi to assert control over the entire nation and establish a new dynasty. This last occurred in 1949 when the Communist forces sailed across the Yangzi in a great

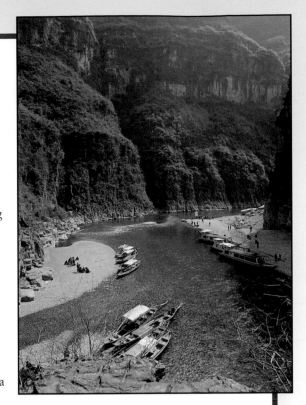

fleet of junks to capture the Nationalist capital of Nanjing.

Now, after generations of tragic upheavals, China is enjoying a period of unprecedented peace and prosperity. The Dragon is molting and the river is in transformation. The continuing 'reform and opening' of China has borne dramatic changes in the economic and personal lives of its people. The Chinese are rediscovering traditional values and customs even as they rush headlong into modernization with all its intractable problems.

A journey on the Yangzi is full of contrasts: ancient walled towns and grandiose broadcast towers; delicate bamboo and silk handicrafts and belching factories; backbreaking menial laborers and blaring limousines sharing a common traffic jam; market peddlars hawking and businessmen barking on cellular phones; ancient temples smokey with burnt offerings for the dead and flashing neon nightlife. Socialist feudalism is giving way to the Age of Karaoke Comm-Fucianism.

The river valley is home to some 500 million people and produces a bounty of foods, goods and services—from herbal medicine in Tibet to computer chips in Shanghai. This 'land of fish and rice' feeds the nation and exports myriad products, including its indigenous contributions of tea, silk and porcelain. The Yangzi Valley is the focus of major national investment like the giant Boshan steel complex near Shanghai, new highways and dam projects.

The river is also bearing the brunt of increasing pollution, ship traffic, agricultural run off and heavy silt from the extensive deforestation of eastern Tibet. Many native species are under threat from extinction—pandas, large river sturgeon, pink river dolphins, alligators and giant salamanders. An ever-growing stream of waste, debris and toxins makes some stretches of the river look like an open sewer. The government environmental regulations are often ignored as the population grows and prosperity overrides protection. A comprehensive bio-diversity survey of the Three Gorges has yet to be made.

The first dam across the Yangzi, the Gezhouba at Yichang, and the immense new Three Gorges Dam, currently under construction, will forever change this magnificent region and its ecology all the way to the sea. This new dam is an environmental sacrifice for the much needed benefits of electrical power, flood control and navigation. It promises to open ocean shipping to Sichuan, a major boost to the economy of the province's 110 million residents. As the world's largest construction project the dam is fraught with serious engineering, social and financial challenges. It may never realize its benefits but may, instead, prove to be an unprecedented danger.

If the project continues as planned, by the year 2003, the river will have a great reservoir 600 kilometers long. The banks and canyons of the Gorges will be inundated, requiring the relocation of approximately 1,500,000

residents. Its indigenous inhabitants, the Tujia people, or 'People of the Earth', descendants of the Ba Kingdom, will lose their ancestral land.

The construction of new roads, towns and agricultural terraces has already begun, preparing for the rising waters. Salvage archaeology has yielded a wealth of artifacts; some are now on display in a new museum in the city of Wanxian. When flooded, the Gorges will have new vistas and human interest while the scenic drama of their natural state will be part of the past.

Future generations will look back at the end of the Twentieth Century when the 'Great Wall across the Yangzi' was built and remember the natural and cultural heritage of the river. They will, one hopes, judge this project as a monumental benefit to the people of China, not just as a disaster of state planning. Will the Great River, like Chinese civilization, long flowing and surviving many troubles, still sustain a wealth of life, and endure?

The officers and staff of Victoria Cruises invite you to experience the Yangzi and its people for yourself. The Victoria fleet is an American and Chinese joint venture that established the first onboard Western management of ships in China. It is our pleasure to provide the best facilities, cuisine, service, education and local cultural entertainment on the Yangzi. Our traditional Chinese hospitality will enhance your enjoyment of the magnificent vistas, fascinating history and vibrant contemporary life of the Great River. Welcome aboard!

Victoria Cruises Incorporated, 57-08 39th Avenue, Woodside, NY 11377, USA
Tel: 212-818-1680 or 800-348-8084 Fax: 212-818-9889

Copyright © 1997, 1995, 1989, 1985 The Guidebook Company Ltd, Hong Kong
All maps copyright © 1997 The Guidebook Company Ltd, Hong Kong
Revised 1997. Reprinted 1998
Odyssey Guides, an imprint of The Guidebook Company Ltd,
G/F 2 Lower Kai Yuen Lane, North Point, Hong Kong
Tel. 852 2856 3896   Fax. 852 2565 8624
E mail: odyssey@asiaonline.net

Distribution in the United Kingdom, Ireland and Europe by
Hi Marketing Ltd, 38 Carver Road, London SE24 9LT, UK
ISBN: 962-217-479-5

Although the publisher and author of this book have made every effort to ensure the
information was correct at the time of going to press, the publisher and author do not
assume and hereby disclaim any liability to any party for any loss or damage caused by
errors, omissions or misleading information.

Grateful acknowledgement is made to the authors and publishers for permissions granted:

Alfred A Knopf, Inc and Brook Hersey for *A Single Pebble* by John Hersey © 1956, 1984,
1989 First Vintage Books; Houghton Mifflin Co, Aitken, Stone & Wylie Ltd and Michael
Russell Ltd for *Sailing Through China* by Paul Theroux © 1983, 1984; Jonathan Cape Ltd
for *Birdless Summer* by Han Suyin © 1968; Penguin for *Poems of the Late T'ang* translated
by A C Graham © 1985; Foreign Language Press, Beijing for *Mao, Swimming in the Yangzi*.

Editor of this edition: Kevin Bishop
Map Design: Tom Le Bas, Bai Yiliang and Au Yeung Chui Kwai
Cover Concept: Aubrey Tse
With special thanks to William Hurst and Richard Hayman for their invaluable assistance
and contributions

Photographs and illustrations:
Magnus Bartlett 57; Kevin Bishop 143, 167; sketches by Bobby Chan 27; Teresa Coleman
Fine Arts Ltd 101, 122; La Grande Artère de La Chine: Le Yangtseu, Joseph Dautremer 65;
GEOPIC™ images, ©Earth Satellite Corporation 4–5, 52–53; Hong Kong China Tourism
Photo Library, back cover, 37, 68, 138, 170; William Lindesay 109, 114; Tom Nebbia 80–
81, 130–131; R Wada 48; Wattis Fine Art 166; How Man Wong, front cover, 1, 8–9, 13,
17, 28, 61, 77, 84–85, 105, 118, 134–135, 175; Sydney Wong 44

Production by Twin Age Limited, Hong Kong
Printed in Hong Kong

(*Previous page*) *Near the source of the Yangzi River at over 5,000 metres,*
high in the Qinghai-Tibetan Plateau

THE
YANGZI RIVER

Judy Bonavia
Revised by William Hurst

Chongming Island

Shanghai

Huangpu River

Contents

*(preceding pages) GEOPIC™ photograph of the Yangzi River entering
the East China Sea just north of Shanghai, taken in 1978*

The River's Source

From the bitter cold and treeless alps of Upper Qinghai, around the source of the Yangzi, the snow that gradually melts in the summer sun trickles down the beds of ancient glaciers, and finally reaches the pastures where man and beast can survive. The snowmelt forms small streams which sing through the tilted plateaus and nourish the grassroots and the hardy little flowers and plants, which the local Tibetan people use as medicine for a variety of ills.

The streams flow more swiftly down the lower Qinghai mountains, which give an impression of Central Europe. On successive steps of mountain and plateau, the people of the Yushu Tibetan Autonomous District cultivate barley and shelter the herds in winter, sending them up to the high pastures only in spring. Their diet consists of meat, milk (fresh and fermented), and barley-meal, which is the staple. Sometimes they add sugar brought from distant parts of China. And in the forest belts they cut timber for the construction of new towns.

The ubiquitous yak is the most useful beast, but sheep are reared for meat and wool and there are some goats. The tough, shaggy little ponies of the mountains are used as a means of transport, and mares' milk is a treasured delicacy and cure-all.

Animal husbandry is the main occupation of these Tibetans and they continue to lead a semi-nomadic life, living in thick black yak-hair tents lined with bags of precious barley, and surrounded by their grazing flocks. For several days each spring the people gather together to sing, dance, hold horse races and tugs of war, before again returning to their lives of isolation.

The streams turn to sizeable rivers as they come down to the 3,000-metre (10,000-foot) level or thereabouts. Typically they flow blue and wide across valley floors where the barley is now fairly abundant and small villages—decorated with the inevitable Buddhist prayer flags—take the place of tent encampments. Despite their deep poverty, the women dress gaily in black and a rainbow of decorative colours, plaiting their hair almost like Africans, and wearing it in braids, sometimes interwoven with red cord. To commemorate special religious festivals, pilgrimages are made to monasteries (often many days' riding away) for they are social as well as religious occasions.

The wildlife is abundant—Tibetan antelopes, Mongolian gazelles, snow leopards, otters, martens, lynxes and deer as well as dozens of species of birds. Carp throng the cold waters of the lakes. Nature reserves are being established to protect the beautiful and threatened snow leopard and the primeval forests in which the wild ass and the snow cock still roam.

(previous pages) At over 5,000 metres sheep graze near the tongue of one of the glaciers whose meltwaters feed the upper Tuotuohe in western Qinghai Province on the border with Tibet. For several years this river was considered to be the source of the Yangzi

Getting There

The Three Gorges, which lie between Chongqing and Yichang, are the most popular destination for tourists.

Chongqing in Sichuan Province is the normal starting point for the downriver Yangzi cruises. Boat departures are normally early in the morning so it is usually necessary to spend the night in Chongqing. The journey through the Three Gorges to Yichang and on downstream to Wuhan takes three-and-a-half days, while the upriver journey, from Wuhan to Chongqing, takes four-and-a-half days.

Scheduled Passenger Boats

Regular passenger boats (*ban chuan*) travel all the way to Shanghai. However, it should be noted that most of these boats terminate at either Yichang or Wuhan, and it is therefore necessary to book onward passages at these stops. There are ticket offices at the piers. Depending on the type of boat and its schedule, the 1,125-kilometre (700-mile) journey between Wuhan and Shanghai may take up to four days upstream and three days downstream.

There are daily sailings of these scheduled passenger boats in both directions from Wuhan, Nanjing and Shanghai. They serve all the Yangzi towns and indeed, for many of these towns, the boats are the only viable means of long-distance transport, since the ports are not all connected by motorable roads. Fares vary with the distance travelled.

■ SCHEDULED SERVICES, WUHAN–CHONGQING–WUHAN

Going upstream from Wuhan, not only are there more ports of call, but the journey takes about 100 hours (four nights on board) compared with 57 hours (two nights on board) going downstream. Not every sailing makes the same stops, but the timetable below shows the main daily service on this run. Additional daily sailings make scheduled stops at towns not included in the downstream schedule shown below.

Conditions on different steamers also vary; the East is Red Shipping Company may have updated its name to Golden Line, but it has scarcely modernized the rustier vessels in its fleet. Most of them, though, have four classes of accommodation starting with second class (there is no first class). Second class consists of two-birth cabins furnished with bedding, a desk, two chairs and a wash basin. On some boats there is also a communal sitting room for viewing. Third class provides ten-person accommodation in two-tiered bunks; fourth class is similar, with bunks for twelve or more persons; in fifth class passengers are packed into masses of three-tiered bunks.

At mealtimes an insistent loudspeaker system announces sittings in the steamer's huge and chaotic dining room. You need to buy a meal ticket in advance. Bottled soft drinks and snacks (biscuits, nuts and so on) are sold in the vicinity of the dining room. On some ships a separate dining room for second-class passengers makes feeding less of a fight, but it is always a good idea to bring some of your own food. There is an unceasing supply of hot boiled water, trickling in a mud-laden stream, from a tap somewhere on board.

MAIN PASSENGER SHIPPING TIMETABLE:
WUHAN (HANKOU TERMINAL)–CHONGQING (UPSTREAM)
CHONGQING–WUHAN (DOWNSTREAM)

UPSTREAM		PORT	DOWNSTREAM	
Arrival	Departure	Port	Arrival	Departure
	09:00	Hankou	16:00	
21:00	21:30	Chenglingji	07:30	08:00
	(second day)		(third day)	
12:00	12:30	Shashi	23:00	23:30
18:00	18:30	Zhicheng	19:30	20:00
22:00	23:00	Yichang	17:00	17:30
	(third day)			
10:30	11:00	Badong	11:45	12:15
			(second day)	
15:00	15:30	Wushan		
18:10	18:40	Fengjie		
23:10	23:40	Yunyang		
	(fourth day)			
09:00	11:30	Wanxian	18:00	04:35
17:50	18:20	Zhongxian		
21:20	21:40	Gaojiazhen		
23:15	23:40	Fengdu		
	(fifth day)			
03:30	04:00	Fuling	11:30	12:00
12:20		Chongqing		07:00

Tickets for this portion may be bought through branches of China International Travel Service and China Travel Service in Chongqing and Wuhan (for addresses, see pages 173 and 177) or direct from Chaotianmen docks (opposite Wharf 2) in Chongqing and the Yangzi Passenger Terminal (80 Yanjiang Dadao) in Hankou, Wuhan. They are sold up to four days in advance of the sailing.

CRUISE BOATS

A more luxurious way of seeing the Three Gorges is to book on one of the many cruise ships catering mainly to foreign tour groups. Most sail the stretch to and from Chongqing–Yichang, or as far as Wuhan. Two new deluxe cruise lines, Regal China Cruises and Victoria Cruises, also offer longer trips, some as long as nine nights, sailing from Shanghai to Chongqing, for instance. The boats operate from the end of March or the beginning of April to October or November. Fitted out with private bathrooms for each cabin, air-conditioning, observation decks, gift shops and bars, these ships offer arranged excursions on shore and other entertainments during the three to four-day cruise.

Many international travel companies run China tours which include a Yangzi River cruise on one of these deluxe ships, including Abercrombie and Kent, who have long been famous for deluxe cruises on the river. China Travel Service runs a week-long tour from Chongqing to Wuhan, which begins and ends in Hong Kong (for addresses see page 171–2). Bookings for all Yangzi cruises should be made well in advance, particularly for September and October, which is the peak tourist season. Although most people take these cruises as part of a group tour, it is also possible to buy individual tickets for the cruise only.

The Yangzi is navigable from Shanghai to Xinshezhen in Sichuan—a distance of over 3,000 kilometres. Yangzi captains must keep a constant vigil and consider the Great River far more hazardous than mere ocean navigation

GETTING TO CHONGQING
■ BY AIR
China Travel Air Service Hong Kong, a subsidiary of China Travel Service Hong Kong (*see* page 172 for address), runs daily charter flights from and to Hong Kong, except for Fridays and Sundays. Within China, there are daily flights from Beijing, Shanghai, Guangzhou and Chengdu. There are also flights to Chongqing from Beihai, Changsha, Dalian, Fuzhou, Haikou, Harbin, Kunming, Nanjing, Shantou, Shenyang, Shenzhen, Urumqi, Wuhan, Xiamen and Xi'an.

■ BY RAIL
Chongqing is accessible by train from all major cities in China, with changes where appropriate. The most common routes are from Kunming via Chengdu, Guilin via Guiyang, and by a direct service from Beijing.

GETTING TO YICHANG
■ BY AIR
At present, flights to Yichang operate twice-weekly from Guangzhou and also Shashi, and once a week from Xi'an. There are also daily flights from Wuhan.
    The air network has been supplemented by China Tourism Charter Air Service Company (with an agency in Yichang) which plans to charter flights to some 18 cities from Dangyang Airfield. CITS and CTS are the best sources for information on these flights.

■ BY RAIL
Trains run several times daily between Yichang and Wuhan.

GETTING TO WUHAN
■ BY AIR
CTS's subsidiary, China Travel Air Service Hong Kong (*see* page 172) runs daily charter flights from and to Hong Kong. Within China, there are daily flights from Beijing, Shanghai, Guangzhou and Yichang. There are also flights to Wuhan from Baotou, Changzhou, Chengdu, Chongqing, Fuzhou, Haikou, Hangzhou, Harbin, Huhot, Kunming, Lanzhou, Nanjing, Ningbo, Qingdao, Shantou, Shashi, Shenyang, Shenzhen, Tianjin, Wenzhou, Xi'an and Yantai.

■ BY RAIL
Wuhan is 18 hours from Beijing and about 24 hours from Guangzhou. There are also direct trains between Wuhan and Yichang, Chengdu, Xi'an, Tianjin, Qingdao, Guilin and Zhenjiang.

Facts for the Traveller

Climate

The three large cities along the Yangzi River—Chongqing, Wuhan and Nanjing—are known traditionally as the 'three furnaces of China'. Between April and September, the temperature in the Yangzi River valley reaches 36°C (97°F) and above. Spring and autumn are therefore the best seasons for making the river cruises. However, with the tall mountains and gorges through which the river threads its path, precipitation is very high and the peaks are often shrouded in cloud and mist, although a light haze can enhance the beauty of the scenery. Summer rains are torrential; you may find dramatic thunderstorms comforting if you are on board your boat but a nuisance should you be trying to sightsee ashore. The winters are short, cold and crisp. Late-summer travels will coincide with the high-water periods, when the river rises swiftly, almost perceptibly.

CHONGQING
AVERAGE TEMPERATURES

	Jan	Feb	Mar	Apr	May	Jun	Jul	Aug	Sep	Oct	Nov	Dec
°C	7	10	14.5	19.5	23	25.5	29	30	25	19	14	10.5
°F	44.6	50	58.1	67.1	73.4	77.9	84.2	86	77	66.2	57.2	50.9

AVERAGE RAINFALL

	Jan	Feb	Mar	Apr	May	Jun	Jul	Aug	Sep	Oct	Nov	Dec
mm.	15	20	38	99	142	180	142	122	150	112	48	20
in.	0.6	0.8	1.5	3.9	5.6	7.1	5.6	4.8	5.9	4.4	1.9	0.8

WUHAN
AVERAGE TEMPERATURES

	Jan	Feb	Mar	Apr	May	Jun	Jul	Aug	Sep	Oct	Nov	Dec
°C	2.7	5.2	10	16.2	21.1	26.1	29.1	28.4	23.9	17.6	11.4	5.5
°F	36.8	41.3	50	61.1	69.9	79.8	84.3	83.1	75	63.6	52.5	41.9

AVERAGE RAINFALL

	Jan	Feb	Mar	Apr	May	Jun	Jul	Aug	Sep	Oct	Nov	Dec
mm.	152	152	203	279	305	381	254	203	178	178	152	127
in.	6	6	8	11	12	15	10	8	7	7	6	5

Clothing

Light summer clothing is all that is required between April and September, with a woollen cardigan or warm jacket for the cool evenings on board. To combat the summer mugginess, travellers should wear cotton rather than synthetic fibres. Those who rise at dawn to watch the passage through the gorges may imitate the Chinese passengers who huddle in blankets supplied by the ship.

The Yangzi River towns are very informal indeed; wear comfortable everyday clothes when you visit them. Steep steps from the jetties to the towns require walking shoes, and since the streets turn to mud within minutes of a heavy rainfall, you may need an extra pair. Umbrellas can be bought cheaply almost anywhere. On board the more deluxe ships, however, many like to dress a little more formally for the last night of the cruise; therefore women may want to bring a smart outfit and men a jacket and tie.

Warm clothes are essential for the river journeys during seasons other than summer. The boats can be draughty and the wind piercing. However clothing is one of the best bargains in China, with excellent down or quilt jackets available in many of the big towns and cities. Bring a pair of light hiking boots as the terrain can be hilly, rocky and muddy.

Visas

Everyone must get a visa to go to China, but this is usually a trouble-free process. Tourists travelling in a group are listed on a single group visa issued in advance to the travel agent involved. Their passports will not be individually stamped with the visa or on arrival and departure unless specifically requested.

Tourist visas for individual travellers can be obtained at Chinese embassies and consulates as well as from certain travel agents in your respective countries; from the Chinese Ministry of Foreign Affairs visa office in Hong Kong (the cheapest way) or through several Hong Kong travel agents including branches of CTS (see page 172). It is simplest in Hong Kong. The application procedure is quite routine; you simply fill in a form, supply one photograph and hand in a fee with your passport.

Visa fees vary considerably depending on the source of the visa and on the time taken to get it. In Hong Kong, for instance, you can get a single-entry three-month tourist visa within one working day (application handed in at 9 am and collected at 4.30 pm) for around US$40, while a visa processed in 72 hours might cost half that.

Money

CHINESE CURRENCY

Chinese currency is called Renminbi (meaning 'people's currency') and this is abbreviated to Rmb. It is denominated in *yuan*, referred to as *kuai* in everyday speech. The *yuan* is divided into 10 *jiao* (colloquially called *mao*). Each *jiao* is divided into 10 *fen*. There are large notes for 100, 50, 5, 2 and 1 *yuan*, small notes for 5,2, and 1 *jiao*, and coins and notes for 5, 2, 1 *fen* and 1 *yuan*. Foreign Exchange Certificates (FECs) have now been abolished; Rmb is now convertible only in China and Hong Kong.

FOREIGN CURRENCY, TRAVELLER'S CHEQUES AND CREDIT CARDS

There is no limit to the amount of foreign currency you can take into China. Travellers' cheques are changed at a slighter better rate than cash. All major European, American and Japanese travellers' cheques are accepted by the Bank of China. International credit cards may be used in a limited number of Friendship Stores, hotels and banks, but check with your credit card company or bank.

TIPPING

Tipping is officially forbidden in China. However, in the larger cities—Beijing,

Leshan Buddha, Sichuan—the world's largest stone sculpture
cut in the 8th century during the Tang dynasty

Shanghai and Guangzhou for example—the practice is becoming acceptable, and service staff in the joint-venture hotels, guides and drivers will generally welcome tips.

BARGAINING

With the exception of state-run stores with fixed prices, always bargain in markets and shops. Even state-run stores will sometimes give discounts on expensive items like carpets. Bargaining in China can be good-humoured or it can be infuriating; it is a game won by technique and strategy, not by anger or threats. Thus, it should be leisurely and friendly, and not be seen as a one-way process at all, since the Chinese enjoy it. Finally, it is bad manners to continue to bargain after a deal has been struck.

Travel Agencies

A number of state-owned corporations handle foreign visitors to China and foreign tour operators make most arrangements through them. The largest is China International Travel Service (CITS), whose offices are located in most Chinese cities and which also has representative offices abroad. Other large nationwide organizations providing similar services are China Travel Service (CTS) and China Youth Travel Service (CYTS). Formerly CITS handled only foreign travellers, while overseas Chinese were looked after by CTS. With recent policy changes, this distinction no longer exists.

CITS offers a comprehensive service covering accommodation, transportation, food and sightseeing. It also provides services such as ticket sales for walk-in customers, for which a handling fee is charged. Many individual travellers have found the service provided at some branch offices wanting; this apparent unhelpfulness can often be put down to a lack of resources, which are generally expended on tour groups. Also, plane, train and boat tickets are in short supply, especially during September and October.

For a select list of foreign tour operators offering Yangzi cruises, see page 171.

Communications

China's post-office system is rather slow but reliable. Every post office counter has a pot of glue, as low-denomination stamps do not have glue on the backs.

International Direct Dialling is available in the big cities along the river, such as Chongqing, Yichang and Wuhan, although it is often difficult to get through.

Long-distance telephone calls within China take much longer to connect than international ones (sometimes hours) and often have very bad lines. Many new hotels have telex and fax facilities.

Local Time

Amazingly for a country measuring 3,220 kilometres (over 2,000 miles) from east to west, the whole of China operates from one time zone 8 hours ahead of GMT and 13 hours ahead of EST. China has experimented with summer time, but abandoned it in 1992.

Packing Checklist

As well as bringing along any prescription medicines you may need, it is a good idea to pack a supply of common cold and stomach trouble remedies. While it is not necessary to pack toilet paper these days, it is advisable to take some with you when going out sightseeing, as public toilets do not provide it. Bring plenty of film and camera accessories, such as batteries and flashes. Although film is widely available, the right type may not always be obtainable at the right time. Comfortable, non-slip shoes are a must

Health

There are no mandatory vaccination requirements. However, you may be advised by your doctor to take certain precautions. In recent years the US Consulate in Hong Kong has recommended inoculations against hepatitis A and B, Japanese encephalitis B, tetanus, polio, cholera and malaria. The risk of contracting any of these diseases is small, although it increases during the summer months and in rural areas. To minimize risks, remember to drink only mineral or boiled water, make sure all food is freshly cooked and peel all fruit. Most tourist cruise ships have doctors on board.

The Course of the Yangzi

XINJIANG AUTONOMOUS REGION

INNER MONGOLIA

QINGHAI

Xining

Lanzhou

GANSU

AUTO
REG

Tuotuo River

BAYAN SHAN

Tongtian River

Damqu River

Yalong River

Dadu River

Min River

Jialing River

Lhasa

TIBET AUTONOMOUS REGION

Jinsha River

DAXUE SHAN

Chengdu

SICHUAN

Chongqing

HIMALAYAS

HENGDUAN SHAN

Emei Shan

DALIANG SHAN

Yibin

Shigu

Guiyan

Kunming

YUNNAN

WULIANG SHAN

0   100   200   300   400   500 km

100   200   300 miles

OMOUS REGION

LIAONING

BEIJING ●

Tianjin

Bo Hai

HEBEI

Shijiazhuang

Weihai

uan

Taiyuan

Yantai

A
JS

SHANXI

Jinan

SHANDONG

Qingdao

Tai Shan

Yellow Sea

SHAANXI

Zhengzhou

Xi'an

Luoyang

HENAN

JIANGSU

Yangzhou

Han River

Nanjing

Zhenjiang

Nantong

DABA SHAN

Hefei

Wuxi

Shanghai

Yunyang

Wushan

Zigui

HUBEI

ANHUI

Ma'anshan

Suzhou

Wanxian

Yichang

Yangzi River

Wuhu

Tai Lake

Fengjie

Badong

Jingzhou

Wuhan

Anqing

Tongling

Hangzhou

Zhong Xian
(Three Gorges)

Shashi

Qizhou

Guichi

Huang Shan

u River

Huangshi

Pengze

ZHEJIANG

uling

Jiujiang

Hukou

Jinhua

Lu Shan

East
China
Sea

Dongting Lake

Poyang Lake

HAN

River

Nanchang

u River

Changsha

Gan River

Heng Shan

JIANGXI

ZHOU

HUNAN

Xiang River

Fuzhou

Guilin

FUJIAN

Taipei

ANGXI ZHUANGZU
TONOMOUS REGION

GUANGDONG

Taiwan Strait

TAIWAN

Nanning

Guangzhou

Macau

Hong Kong

South China Sea

© The Guidebook Company Ltd

The Yangzi River: An Introduction

The mighty Yangzi, or Changjiang, is the third largest river in the world. (The Nile is the longest, followed by the Amazon.) At 6,300 kilometres (3,900 miles), the Yangzi is closest in length to the Mississippi. Among the Chinese, the name Yangzi is not as commonly used as Changjiang—simply, Long River.

This extensive waterway cuts through the heart of China, and is regarded by the Chinese as marking the division of their country into north and south, both geographically and culturally. The river rises in the far western part of China and flows through eight provinces before disgorging its waters into the Yellow Sea. Over 700 tributaries draining a further six provinces join the Yangzi along its course.

The Yangzi is divided into three parts:

The Upper Reaches from the source in Qinghai Province to Yichang in Hubei Province, a distance of some 4,400 kilometres (2,700 miles). This stretch is one of great beauty, with wild mountain ranges, unbroken ravines, unnavigable rapids and rushing torrents. The Three Gorges are included in this section, as is the Sichuan Basin.

The Middle Reaches from Yichang to Hukou at the mouth of Poyang Lake in Jiangxi Province, a distance of about 1,000 kilometres (620 miles). Here, the river widens and flows through flat, low-lying land and and is fed by waters from two huge lakes, the Dongting and the Poyang. This is the region where the battle against flooding has been carried on for centuries; earthen dikes and paved embankments tell of past and present heroic struggles.

The Lower Reaches from Hukou to the estuary, a distance of some 900 kilometres (560 miles). The landscape in the river's lower course is typified by a flat delta plain crisscrossed by canals and waterways, with soil so rich and water so abundant that the region has been known for centuries as the 'Land of Fish and Rice'.

The wet season begins in April, bringing heavy rain in the middle and lower reaches. By July and August the wet weather reaches the Sichuan Basin where the prevalence of mountainous terrain causes widespread rainfall. Then, as the water level starts to subside, the 'Sichuan waters' begin to threaten again.

The rich Yangzi River Basin, according to current statistics, produces 40 per cent of the national grain (including 70 per cent of all paddy rice), one-third of the country's cotton, 48 per cent of its freshwater fish and 40 per cent of the total industrial output value. Its hydroelectric energy potential is almost boundless: Gezhouba Dam at Yichang is one of the biggest low-water dams in the world and the planned Three Gorges Dam will be the world's largest hydroelectric project. One-third of China's 1.1 billion people live in this prosperous basin, which also boasts a rich cultural heritage.

One would imagine from the impressive statistics that the river would be choked with vessels of all descriptions, but this is not the case. Ocean-going ships do frequent the river from Wuhan down, but the traffic consists mainly of ferry boats, lighters, barges, tugs and logging rafts. Over the years, political instability had taken its toll on economic development, but it was the building of railways in the hinterland that really changed the life of the river. When rail freight proved to be cheaper than transportation along the Yangzi and its tributaries, the heyday of river transport was over.

Attempts are being made to revitalize the river transport system. Studies point out that it is cheaper to dredge than to build branch railways. Over three billion *yuan* of state investment has been fed into the Yangzi shipping industry over the last 40 years. When the Three Gorges Dam is built, the watercourse through the Gorges will be deeper and safer, allowing larger vessels to sail to and from Chongqing.

Table of Distances Between Main Yangzi River Ports

Distances in kilometres (miles)

Chongqing	Chongqing										
Wanxian	327 (203)	Wanxian									
Fengjie	446 (277)	119 (74)	Fengjie								
Yichang	648 (403)	321 (200)	202 (126)	Yichang							
Shashi	815 (506)	488 (303)	369 (229)	167 (104)	Shashi						
Wuhan	1354 (841)	1027 (638)	908 (564)	706 (439)	539 (335)	Wuhan					
Jiujiang	1623 (1008)	1296 (805)	1177 (731)	975 (606)	806 (502)	269 (167)	Jiujiang				
Wuhu	1991 (1237)	1664 (1034)	1545 (960)	1343 (835)	1176 (731)	637 (396)	368 (229)	Wuhu			
Nanjing	2087 (1297)	1760 (1094)	1641 (1020)	1439 (894)	1272 (790)	733 (455)	464 (288)	96 (60)	Nanjing		
Zhenjiang	2174 (1351)	1847 (1148)	1728 (1074)	1526 (948)	1359 (844)	820 (510)	551 (342)	183 (114)	87 (54)	Zhenjiang	
Shanghai	2479 (1540)	2152 (1337)	2023 (1263)	1831 (1138)	1664 (1034)	1125 (699)	856 (532)	488 (303)	392 (244)	305 (190)	Shanghai

BOATS GREAT AND SMALL   —by Judy Bonavia

The traditional Chinese boats that navigated the Yangzi were *sanpans* (meaning three planks), the larger-sized *wupans* (five planks) and junks. Their sails were tall to capture any welcome breeze, and stiffened by bamboo battens. The sculling oar, or *yuloh*, was extremely long with normally four men working it. Mats overhead provided shelter for passengers; decks were covered with coils of bamboo rope. Local pilots were hired to negotiate the most difficult rapids. Their instructions were relayed to the harnessed trackers pulling the long hauling ropes—often far ahead of the boat—by a drum beaten at different rhythms. Large freight junks often required 300 or 400 trackers as well as groups of strong swimmers who would loosen the ropes should they snag on rocks along the way.

An eighth-century poem gives a compelling picture of the gruelling drudgery of a boat puller's life:

A Boatman's Song
Oh, it's hard to grow up at the way-station side!
The officials've set me to pullin' station boats;
Painful days are more, happy days are few,
Slippin' on water, walkin' on sand, lake birds of the sea;
Against the wind, upstream, a load of ten thousand bushels—
Ahead, the station's far away; behind, it's water everywhere!
Midnight on the dikes, there's snow and there's rain,
From up top our orders: you still have to go again!
Our clothes are wet and cold beneath our short rain cloaks,
Our hearts're broke, our feet're split, how can we stand the pain?
Till break of dawn we suffer, there's no one we can tell,
With one voice we trudge along, singing as we pull;
A thatch-roofed house, what's it worth,
When we can't get back to the place of our birth!
I would that this river turn to farm plots,
And long may we boatmen stop cursing our lots.
                         Wang Qian (768 833)

They were truly beasts of burden, as observed by an American, William L Hall, and his wife, who spent several weeks on a small Chinese cargo-boat in 1922:

If the boat happens to turn about when it is struck by a cross-current, a call from the pilot brings all the trackers to their knees or makes them dig their toes into the dirt. Another call makes them either claw the earth or catch their fingers over projecting stones. Then they stand perfectly still to hold the boat. When it is righted, another call makes them let up gradually and then begin again their hard pull.

Passengers usually took *kuaize*—large *wupans*—and paid for the Yichang–Chongqing trip 185 cash for every 100 *li* (18 cents for every 50 kilometres, or 30 miles). They would also supply wine for the crew, and incense and fireworks for a propitious journey. Going upriver, this journey used to take as long as 40–50 days in the high-water period and 30 days in low water, depending on the size of the boat, while the downriver trip could be completed in 5–12 days. At the end of the journey the passengers might buy some pork as a feast for the crew.

River life was varied along the Yangzi and its tributaries. Big junks, fitted out as theatres, sailed between the towns to give performances of Chinese opera or juggling. Some boats were built as hotels, offering accommodation to travellers arriving too late at night to enter the city gates. Others were floating restaurants and tea-houses, not to mention boats which were a source of livelihood as well as home to the numerous fisherfolk and their families.

Peasants along the lower and middle Yangzi first set eyes on foreign men-of-war and steamers when Britain's Lord Elgin journeyed as far as Wuhan (Han-kow) in 1842. Although the Chinese had in fact invented the paddle wheel (worked probably by the treadmill system) for driving their battleships as early as the eighth century, paddle boats were not widely used. In an incident on Dongting Lake in 1135, they were proved positively useless when the enemy threw straw matting on the water and brought the paddle wheels to a stop. They seem not to have been used since.

With the opening up of the Yangzi ports to foreign trade in the latter half of the 19th century, foreign shallow draught paddle steamers and Chinese junks worked side by side. But the traditional forms of river transport slowly became obsolete, and were confined to the Yangzi tributaries for transporting goods to the distribution centres.

Early Western shipping on the Shanghai–Wuhan stretch of the river was dominated by Americans, whose experience of paddle steamers on the Mississippi and other rivers had put them to the fore. The American firm of Russell and Company was the leading shipping and trading concern in those years. A fifth of the foreign trade was in opium shipped up to Wuhan. By the late 1860s, British companies such as Jardine & Matheson and Butterfield & Swire had successfully challenged the American supremacy. Accommodation on the companies' river boats was luxurious, and trade was brisk.

The Wuhan–Yichang stretch was pioneered by an English trader, Archibald Little, who established a regular passenger service in 1884 with his small steamer *Y-Ling*. In his book *Through the Yang-tse Gorges*, he described the bustling scene on the river:

The lively cry of the trackers rings in my ears, and will always be associated in my mind with the rapids of the Upper Yang-tse. This cry is 'Chor-Chor', said to mean 'Shang-chia', or 'Put your shoulder to it', 'it' being the line which is slung over the shoulder of each tracker, and attached to the quarter-mile-long tow-rope of plaited bamboo by a hitch, which can be instantaneously cast off and rehitched. The trackers mark time with this cry, swinging their arms to and fro at each short step, their bodies bent forward, so that their fingers almost touch the ground. . . Eighty or a hundred men make a tremendous noise at this work, almost drowning the roar of the rapids, and often half a dozen junks' crews are towing like this, one behind the other. From the solemn stillness of the gorge to the lively commotion of a rapid, the contrast is most striking.

Other companies soon followed, but none dared travel this route at night. Again, it was Archibald Little's perseverance that brought about steamship navigation through the gorges above Yichang to Chongqing. Acting as captain and engineer, he successfully navigated his 17-metre (55-foot) *Leechuan* up to Chong-qing in 1898, though he still needed trackers to pull him over the worst rapids.

During the heyday of the Yangzi in the 1920s and 1930s, travel by steamer from Shanghai all the way up to Chongqing was luxurious though not entirely safe. Halfway, at Wuhan, passengers had to change to smaller boats for the rest of the journey.

After the establishment of the People's Republic of China, emphasis was placed on making the Yangzi safe for navigation all year round, and all the major obstructions were blown up. The Yangzi today is still a vital artery. Many river towns are almost entirely dependent on it for connecting them to each other. The regular ferries and boats, offering a range of accommodation, always overflow with passengers. There are also luxury cruise boats which normally ply the Chongqing–Wuhan stretch, for three days downstream and four upstream. There are now more than 30 of these cruise boats, carrying from about 60 to over 200 passengers, and more will be put into service in the next few years.

Lao-Hua-ch'iu, *Sichuan's largest type of junk*

Type of Crooked-stern junk (Wai Pigu), specially designed to negotiate sudden twists and turns in the river

Badong Xiao He Huazi (*little river small boat*) *used on the shallow waters of the Little River, a Yangzi tributary upstream from Badong*

Wushan Fan Tail junk (Wushan Shenbozi)

The Upper Reaches:
The Source to Yichang

The melting glaciers and snow fields of the rugged Tanggula Mountains in Qing-hai Province form the headwaters of the Yangzi. It is only since 1976 that the river's true source, the 6,621-metre (21,700-foot) high Mount Geladandong, on the Qinghai-Tibet Plateau, has been conclusively explored and surveyed.

The source of this greatest of China's rivers had long been a geographical conundrum. The area is largely in permafrost, moraine-pitted and wind-swept, an inhospitable and discouraging environment for explorers. A treatise written in the Warring States period (475–221 BC) by geographer Yu Gong stated the source to be in the Mingshan Mountains of Sichuan Province. By the 16th centu-ry, explorers had named Jinsha River in Qinghai as the head stream. In the first half of the 18th century, an official Qing government expedition found its way to the Qinghai–Tibet Plateau; their reports were an impetus for further explora-tions. But it was only when the Changjiang Valley Planning Office sent forth a scientific investigative team in the mid-1970s that the source was finally ascertained.

As the snows melt in the short summer months, waters quietly trickle down to the foothills and flow through the marshes and lakes that form the plateau with its freshly verdant grassland. Among the many rivulets in this region, the Tuotou River emerges as the main body of water, winding its way towards the Qinghai–Tibet Highway and eastwards, for a further 60 kilometres (37 miles), where it is joined by the Damqu River. At this point it becomes the broad upper reaches of the Tongtian River. This plateau abounds in wildlife: Tibetan antelope, wild yaks and asses, lynx and geese.

The 813-kilometre (505-mile) Tongtian River, descending sharply, flows through the Yushu Tibetan Autonomous Region of Qinghai, where the flat lands are cultivated for highland barley or *qingke*—the Tibetan staple diet—and hill slopes provide grazing for the yak, sheep and white-lipped deer owned by Tibet-an herdsmen whose dwellings are black, yak-wool tents. Below the Yushu region the river, navigable here only for short distances by skin coracle boats, becomes known as the Jinsha (Golden Sand) River and flows southwards, forming the border between Tibet and Sichuan on a 2,308-kilometre (1,434-mile) journey sweeping down into Yunnan Province and looping back up into Sichuan. On this southward sweep the Yangzi runs parallel to the upper reaches of the Mekong and Salween Rivers (both of which also rise in the high plateau of Tibet) and the eastern branch of the Irrawaddy. At Shigu (Stone Drum) in Yunnan, the river curves sharply north, actually flowing parallel to itself, separated by only 24

Upper Yangzi River near Lijiang in Yunnan Province, just below Tiger Leaping Gorge. The only access to this valley is via the narrow tracker's path cut into the cliff face on the right.

kilometres (15 miles). Here the river is wide in summer, but in winter, when the water level is low, the currents form sandbars that become the breeding grounds for many varieties of waterbirds. Further on the river again plunges south and east and eventually flows northwards towards Chongqing.

This southern region of the river is an area few Westerners have ever penetrated. In the second half of the 19th century, the British and French sought to establish back-door trade routes from their colonial possessions in Burma, Laos and Vietnam, through Yunnan and up to the navigable stretches of the Yangzi in Sichuan. Secret missions were sent into southwest China, as the British were anxious to study the feasibility of a railway link between Burma and Chongqing. It was these intrepid travellers (some of whom never lived to tell their tale) who recorded their encounters with the many tribal minority peoples inhabiting this area.

Western missionaries were a second source of information on customs and attitudes. But the first Westerner to explore and photograph the area extensively was an American, Joseph F Rock, leader of the National Geographic Society's Yunnan Province Expedition. His amazing black and white photographs, taken in the 1920s and developed by himself under the most difficult conditions, are, even today, outstanding.

Among the sloping forests of pine and spruce are alpine meadows of moss, blue gentians and white edelweiss bordered by hemlock and flowering rhododendron bushes. In the narrow valley floors live tribes of the Tibeto-Burmese ethnic group—the Lisu, Nashi, Lolo (also known as the Yi), Nosu, Lahu, Hsifan and Jing peoples. They have inhabited western Sichuan and northeast Yunnan since earliest times, cultivating barley, wheat, vegetables and indigo and keeping sheep or pigs. For the most part these people are Tibetan Buddhists, but some, like the Nashi, are animists whose priests, or *tombas,* practise exorcism in the pre-Buddhist tradition of the Bon sect of Tibet; others are simply shamanistic. They are brave hunters and warriors, who had fought among themselves and against the Han Chinese for centuries. Until 1949, Buddhist kingdoms, such as the tiny kingdom of Muli, were ruled by reincarnated monk kings.

The Black Yi of Daliang Shan were landowners who kept their fellow tribesmen, the White Yi, as slaves. This practice was proscribed in 1956. The Yi—in their striking long thick black capes—were a constant headache to the Chinese administration, as they kidnapped officials and fomented rebellions. Their exploits were recorded as early as the first century BC by the great Chinese historian Sima Qian (*c.* 145–85 BC). Kublai Khan (1215–94), in an attempt to bring Burma under his sway, lost half his 500,000-man army to disease, exhaustion and tribal harassment in these mountains.

Though the great gorges of the Yangzi near Yichang are the most famous, there are even more spectacular gorges in the vicinity of Lijiang, where mountains rise more than 5,700 metres (18,700 feet) and canyons plunge 3,900 metres (12,800 feet) through which the water flows deeply, turbulently and treacherously.

Access in this region is still only by mountain pathways and cliff-hugging tracks. Single-rope bridges slung high above the water's surface are not uncommon; the rider is conveyed in a sling attached to a pulley which must be well greased with yak butter to avoid any build-up of friction.

The area is rich in mineral resources and timber. The 1,085 kilometre (675-mile) Chengdu–Kunming railway, which was constructed in the 1970s, has brought profound changes to this remote region.

From about the 27 degrees north parallel, the Yangzi, flowing north–northeast for some 800 kilometres (500 miles) and forming the borders of Sichuan and Yunnan, finally reaches the Sichuan or Red Basin. After Yibin, the river, now called the Changjiang, is joined by the Minjiang and Jialing Rivers from the north and the Wujiang from the south. Thus originates the name of Sichuan Province—'Four Rivers'. The 500-metre (1,640-foot) high Sichuan Basin, with its mild winters and long rainy season, has long been agriculturally rich; in the late Han dynasty, Chengdu (today's capital of Sichuan) was even bigger than the then capital of Luoyang. Sichuan has remained one of China's most important 'breadbaskets', producing cotton, hemp and silk as well as grain. On the large flat Chengdu plain, the Minjiang was harnessed for irrigation as early as 250 BC by the Dujiangyan irrigation system, which has been the basis of the region's prosperity ever since.

Near the confluence of the Dadu and Min Rivers is the great sacred Buddhist mountain of Emei, studded with ancient temples. Not far distant, at Leshan, the river actually laps the stone feet of one of the world's largest carved Buddhas. The 70-metre (230-foot) high Tang-dynasty (618–907) statue took 90 years to complete.

The huge city of Chongqing stands at the confluence of the Jialing and the Yangzi. Below this city the river continues its progress through Sichuan, and on through the famous Yangzi Gorges into Hubei Province where, at Yichang, sharply checked by the Gezhouba Dam, it enters the flat lands of its middle reaches.

Chongqing

The "Mountain City" of Chongqing clings to steep cliffs at the confluence of the Yangzi and a major tributary, the Jialing River. This bustling city rises high above docks held in the rushing currents by cables lashed to anchor holes cut into the rocky shore. Cable cars float across to opposite banks and giant bridges carry creeping waves of trucks loaded with the city's varied industrial output. Caves perforate the steep hills, once built as bomb shelters and now busy as garages or naturally cool restaurants and hair salons.

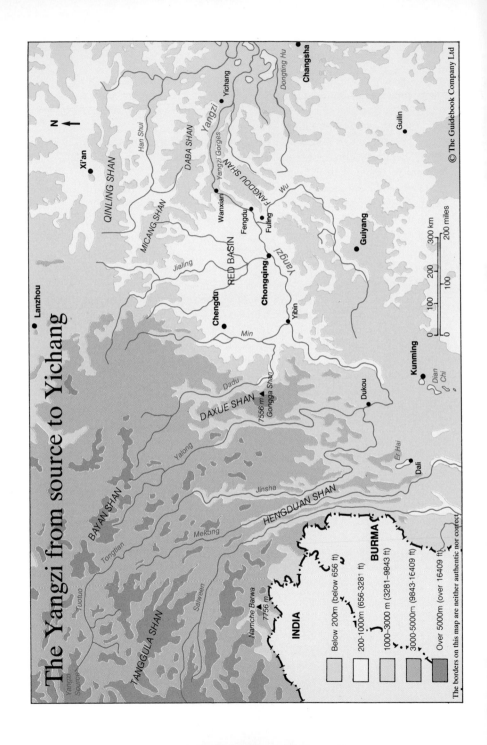

The Yangzi from source to Yichang

N

Below 200m (below 656 ft)

200–1000m (656–3281 ft)

1000–3000 m (3281–9843 ft)

3000–5000m (9843–16409 ft)

Over 5000m (over 16409 ft)

0   100   200   300 km

0   100   200 miles

The borders on this map are neither authentic nor correct

Lanzhou

Xi'an

QINLING SHAN

Han Shui

DABA SHAN

Yangzi

Yichang

Yangzi Gorges

FANGDOU SHAN

MICANG SHAN

Wanxian

Fengdu

Fuling

Wu

RED BASIN

Jialing

Chengdu

Chongqing

Yangzi

Guiyang

Yibin

Min

Changsha

Dongting Hu

Guilin

Kunming

Dian Chi

Dukou

Dadu

DAXUE SHAN

7556 m
Gongga Shan

Er Hai

Dali

Yalong

Jinsha

HENGDUAN SHAN

BAYAN SHAN

Mekong

Tongtian

BURMA

Tuotuo

TANGGULA SHAN

Saiween

Namche Barwa
7756 m

INDIA

Yangzi
Source

For centuries the main commercial and transportation center for Sichuan Province, Chongqing is now under rapid transformation due to the contruction of the Three Gorges Dam. The city was granted national status in 1996 as a municipal region similar to Beijing, Shanghai and Tianjin with an adminstrative region that includes the eastern Sichuan counties downriver for a total population of some 30 million people. Chongqing is now proud to be the world's largest metropolitan region.

This area will bear the brunt and possible benefits of inundation in the world's largest reservoir that will displace over 1.3 million people. Chongqing is already in the midst of vast reconstruction, demolishing many old neighborhoods that had been previously bombed by the Japanese and recontructed into the traditional ramshackle warrens laced with sandstone staircases. These squalid conditions gave close quarters to the city residents who are known for their cheerful pleasure in sitting outside on cool summer nights. The folk cuisine of outdoor sidewalk dining is from *huo guo* or hot pots. These are basins filled with bubbling chili oil and *hua jiao*—flower pepper that cause the mouth to tingle, into which are dipped all kinds of meats and vegetables. Once the river boatmen's campfire meal of leftovers from the day's market, *huo guo* is now the local favorite, sometimes because opium pods are placed in the brew.

Now the traditional lifestyle of Chongqing is being transformed by giant shopping and residential construction complexes that all but eliminate the spicy street life into glitzy boutiques for the parade of newly flush consumers. The center of town is the Jie Fang Bei—a modern tower built to memorialize the martyrs of the civil war—now covered with gaudy advertising. The city is plagued by the worst air pollution in China as industry and traffic jams spew toxins into the humid still air of this landlocked port. The reservoir to come has initiated construction of massive new walls along the river shores with express highways on top to alleviate the thick crawl of traffic through town.

Hundreds of ships line the muddy banks below the remaining old city wall at Chao Tian Men—rusty ferries packed with commuters and barges heaped with goods plying the Three Gorges to the rest of China. Chongqing is the destination for most of the bulk transport that passes through the Gorges, which has been likened to an eyedropper that feeds the elephant of the population of Sichuan at some 120 million. The port bustle is impressive and sweat soaked. Thousands of porters known as the *bang bang jun*—the help army—line up with their bamboo poles and ropes to carry supplies up the staircases. These cheerful troops, some 200,000 on any given day, are farmers on leave from the season in the fields to earn cash in the city. Many also work on the construction sites, camping in the muddy disarray of the crowded city. Compared to the relative clean and urbane cities of China's capital and coast, Chongqing is quite *tu*— earthy and real.

The Bombing of Chongqing

The bombing by the Japanese which began in 1939 continued in 1940 and in 1941 with increasing ferocity. As soon as the winter fogs lifted the planes came, and through the gruelling hot summer, until late in autumn, being bombed was part of the normal process of living. Our daily activities were geared to this predictable occurrence: one rose early, and since the nights were an inferno of heat and sweat, the rock exuding its day-stored heat, it was easy to wake when the sun rose, for dawn did not mean coolness, but another raging hot day. Quickly the fire was lit with sticks of wood and a fan to spurt the flame, water boiled for morning rice, and by nine o'clock the day's first meal (the before-the-bombing meal) had been consumed. The first alert then started. One went to the dugout, with some luggage in hand, kettle and iron pan (irreplaceable after 1940, as metal became almost non-existent); and there one spent the day. Sometimes the bombs fell very near and we came to know the peculiar whistling sound they made. At other times the drone was further away, and the explosions faint. Sometimes the bombers came over five or six times, on occasion up to twenty times a day. And once, in 1941, they continued without let for seven days and nights, and many people died, both in the bombings and also in the air-raid shelters, especially babies, from heat and exhaustion and diarrhoea.

The shelters were scooped-out tunnels in the rock, and since Chungking was all rock, with juttings and small hollows and hillocks almost everywhere, the bowels of these promontories could easily be utilized. But some of the common shelters had been dug in softer earth, and were unsafe. They caved in after a while. There was no ventilation in them, and the people who sat deep inside, away from the one and only outlet, the mouth of the tunnel, became anoxic if the raid was prolonged. They started to thresh about, or to faint. In between the explosions, there was respite. While awaiting the next batch of bombs, everyone would come out of the dugout, sit round the mouth of the cave, fan, gulp the hot air; but this was almost as gruelling as sitting inside the dugout because there was hardly any shade, and if there was a single bush, it was monopolized in its thin narrow coolness by some police squad or some *self-important official and his family. The heat pounded on the rock, the day wore on and on, the hours were a casque of hot lead, were sweat, were suffocation and thirst; a single large wooden bucket was provided for the men to relieve themselves at the mouth of the shelter; nothing was provided for the women. The children could and did squat about, and the area became noisome with smell and flies.*

After 1940 it became dangerous to use a pocket handkerchief to wipe one's sweat during the air raids. There was a rumour that 'spies' had been caught, signalling to the planes with white handkerchiefs. Anyone 'signalling' was to be executed immediately. . . I was witness to one unexplained episode; going to the dugout in our neighbourhood a little late (I always postponed going till the very last minute), I saw a man, hands bound, face covered by a black cloth, with two slits for eyes, being marched off by three soldiers. Behind them came a plain-clothes man holding a revolver loosely, muzzle down. The prisoner would probably be executed in a small private shelter, shot through the back of the neck, and why I did not know. This was another method devised by the secret police for getting rid of 'communists'. The executioner usually took the victim's shoes, after death, to prevent the dead man's ghost running after him.

When we sat outside the shelters, therefore, we had to refrain from showing anything like white cloth, and in the collapsing heat, which never let up, one's skin was always pouring; so we bought towels of grey or blue. When I stood up I would sometimes leave wet marks on the rock where I had been sitting, and that was sweat.

Often, returning home, I found there was no water. The bombings broke the water pipes, and twice hit the Chungking electric plant. Most of Chungking anyway depended on the water-carriers, bringing water from the few mains or from the river two hundred feet below us. Down, down, down and up, up, up, to get a pail of water. . . and this yellow, turbid fluid, the sap of the Great River, cost five, ten dollars a pail. In bad periods I learnt to drink, cook, wash, clean, with only one pail of water a day.

Han Suyin, Birdless Summer, 1968

History of Chongqing

In the fourth century BC, Chongqing (then called Yuzhou) was the capital of the State of Ba, whose men were renowned for their prowess in battle and their military successes. In the Southern Song dynasty (1127–1279) the city's name was changed to Chongqing—meaning 'double celebration'—to mark the princedom and enthronement of Emperor Zhaodun in 1189. He was himself a native of the city.

Chongqing had always been an important port, bustling with junks from Sichuan's hinterlands and neighbouring provinces, and acting as the collection point for the abundant produce of the region, including hides and furs from Tibet, hemp, salt, silk, rhubarb, copper and iron. Under the Qifu Agreement of 1890, Chongqing was opened to foreign trade. This marked the beginning of the exciting history of steamboat navigation from Yichang through the treacherous gorges to Chongqing, a development aimed at opening up the riches of Sichuan to trade with the outside world. By the early part of this century, a massive trade in opium grown in southwest China had sprung up, abetted by warlord factionalism and greed.

Visitors to the city in the 1920s and '30s commented on its 30-metre (100-foot) high city wall, and the rough steps from the river up to the city gates 'dripping with slime from the endless procession of water carriers'. At that time, Chongqing, with a population of over 600,000, had no other water supply. Between ten and twenty thousand coolies carried water daily to shops and houses through the steep and narrow lanes of the city. All porterage was done by coolies as there were no wheeled vehicles in the city, only sedan chairs. The staircase streets are still there, but all that remains of the city wall today is the odd outcrop of masonry that props up a house here, or abuts a path there.

In 1939, during the Sino-Japanese War, the nationalist Guomindang government of China moved the capital from Nanjing to Chongqing, and on the south bank of the Yangzi foreign delegations built substantial quarters, which can be seen from the river. The airstrip used then can still be seen on the Penghu Sandbar as one crosses the Yangzi River Bridge.

The Guomindang government headquarters is now the People's City Government Offices (only the gateway is left of that period), situated just opposite the Renmin Hotel.

During the Sino-Japanese War (1937–45), Chongqing's notorious foggy weather conditions probably saved the city from complete devastation, for only on clear days could the Japanese bombers, which flew over in 20-minute waves, succeed in accurately dropping their thousands of bombs.

What to See in Chongqing

Chongqing, always a trading city, was never noted for its cultural heritage or architecture. However, unlike most northern Chinese cities, Chongqing and other Yangzi River towns are very lively at night. On summer evenings residents stroll about in the hope of a refreshing breeze. Street markets, sidewalk restaurant stalls, herbalists and calligraphers can be found on Wuyi Lu and Bayi Lu. Informal

Chongqing at night

Sichuanese opera can be heard at the **Workers' Park** on Saturday evenings.

The **Chaotianmen Docks** are a fascinating area. Flanked by clothes and noodle stalls, narrow streets thread their way down to the harbour. At the waterfront, a busy panorama unfolds—steamers, tugboats, rows of pontoons, even a cable tramway to ease the ascent from shore to street.

The Jialing cable car starts its journey from Cangbai Lu to Jinsha Jie on the north bank (Jiangbei). The five-minute ride is fun on a clear day. Another cable car, at Wanglongmen, spans the Yangzi to the south.

The **Chongqing Zoo** has several pandas, which are native to Sichuan Province.

■ CHONGQING MUSEUM, 72 PIPASHAN ZHENGJIE

There is a good collection here of earthenware figurines and brick reliefs from the Eastern Han period (AD 25–220). They came from tombs, most likely of wealthy and important men. As was the custom, the deceased were buried with objects recalling the preoccupations of everyday life—farming, hunting and entertainment. While Han tombs were elaborate affairs, the people of Ba, who roamed the plains of Sichuan 2,000 years ago, disposed of their dead in an even more singular fashion, encasing corpses in canoe-shaped wooden coffins and suspending them from cliffs along the river. Two of these huge coffins and the artefacts found inside them are on display here. Open daily, 9 am–12 noon, 2.30–6 pm.

■ THE LUOHAN TEMPLE

This 19th century temple is glimpsed through an ornate passage whose walls are encrusted with rock carvings in the manner of Buddhist grottoes. *Luohan* are Buddhist saints; they traditionally number 500, although in this temple there are actually 524 statues of them. They are of recent vintage, the last of the originals having been destroyed in the Cultural Revolution (1966–76). The present statues were made by the Sichuan Fine Arts Institute in 1985.

■ PAINTERS' VILLAGE (HUAJIA ZHI CUN, LOCATED IN HUALONGQIAO)

Both Painter's Village and the Sichuan Fine Arts Institute (*see below*) are often on tour-group itineraries. However, they are some way out of the city and difficult to reach by public transport. Both establishments have galleries and pieces for sale.

Painters' Village (tel. 52122) was established in the 1950s to nurture artists who would create paintings and lithographs to glorify the revolution. These state-sponsored artists come from all over China and include members of minority nationalities. They are mostly elderly now and enjoy what, for China, are excellent conditions. They have their own studios and produce an impressive range of work. Since China embarked on economic reforms, however, they have had to become commercial, since the government no longer buys all their work.

■ SICHUAN FINE ARTS INSTITUTE (SICHUAN MEISHU XUEYUAN)

This is the only residential undergraduate- and graduate-level fine arts college in southwest China, with a student enrolment of around 300 a year. Students come from all over China as well as from abroad. The college was founded in 1950, and has departments of sculpture, painting, crafts (including lacquerware, textile design, packaging design and ceramics) and teacher training. The institute is particularly proud of its gallery, the largest art-institute gallery in China, which displays the best work of its students. Many of the items are for sale. The institute is located at Huangjiaoping, on the northern bank of the Yangzi, about half-an-hour's drive from the centre of the city. The gallery is open to the public 9 am–12 noon and 2.30–5.30 pm.

■ STILWELL MUSEUM

The museum, which was established in conjunction with the Stilwell Foundation in the USA and the Foreign Affairs Bureau in Chongqing, is dedicated to General Joseph Stilwell and the time he served as commander-in-Chief of the American forces in the 'China-Burma-India theatre', between 1941 and 1945 when the threat of the Japanese Imperial Army was finally overcome. General Stilwell was instrumental in ridding Asia of that threat.

The Museum is located in the actual house occupied by General Stilwell during the war, and is a tribute to his daughters, Alison and Nancy, who devoted so much time and effort in bringing this project to fruition in 1992. Address: 33 Sixin Road. Tel. 770152

■ RED CRAG VILLAGE (HONGYAN CUN) AND GUI YUAN
Both these are now memorial museums to the 1949 revolutionary activities in the city. In the 1930s and '40s, during the period of co-operation between the Guomindang government and the Chinese Communist Party against the aggression of the Japanese, these buildings were the offices of the Communist Party and the Red Army. Mao Zedong stayed in Guiyuan House during his brief stay in Chongqing in 1945.

SIGHTS AROUND CHONGQING

■ SOUTH MOUNTAINS PARK (NANSHAN GONGYUAN)
Situated on the southern side of the Yangzi, this park comprises a scenic group of five mountain peaks of between 400 and 600 metres (1,300 and 2,000 feet) high. On one of these, Yellow Hill (Huangshan), General Chiang Kai-shek, head of the Guomindang government, built his wartime residence. American, British, French and other allied powers also built ambassadorial residences, which are now used as resthouses. The wife of the legendary founder of the Xia dynasty (2205–1766 BC) Emperor Dayu, was said to have lived on another peak, Yu Mountain, in 2200 BC. Dayu, who gained eternal fame for his diligence in harnessing the rivers of China, laboured for 13 years without once returning home. During that time he was said to have 'passed his house three times and never entered', so dedicated was he to his task.

■ NORTHERN HOT SPRINGS (BEIWEN QUAN)
The Northern Hot Springs are some 50 kilometres (30 miles) north of Chongqing, by the bank of the Jialing on Wentang Gorge. Historical records reveal that the Warm Spring Temple existed on this site 1,500 years ago, but the present temple dates from the Ming and Qing dynasties. The four halls rise up the hillside on a central axis. The Guanyin Hall, with iron tiles and stone pillars, is flanked on either side by natural springs. Lotus and fish ponds, ancient trees, bath-houses, restaurants and a guesthouse complete this scenic spot.
    A day's visit to the Northern Hot Springs may also include a visit to the **Beipei Natural History Museum** in which fossil remains of three dinosaurs are exhibited.

■ JINYUN MOUNTAIN
Located near the Northern Hot Springs, the mountain is 1,030 metres (3,380 feet) high and is also known as Little Emei Mountain. Tourists should begin their ascent at Jinyun Temple and climb the 680 steps to Lion's Peak where they may view the nine peaks of Jinyun. The area is a natural botanical garden with 1,700 species of plants and trees.

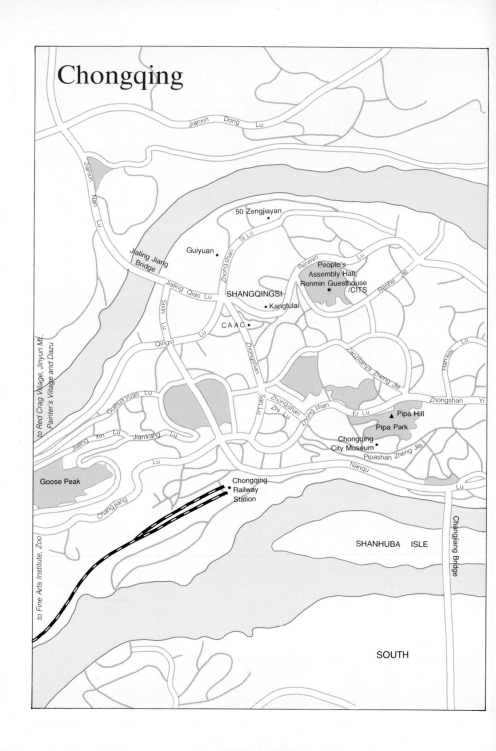

Chongqing

Jianxin Dong Lu

Jianxin Nan Lu

50 Zengjiayan

Guiyuan

Jialing Jiang Bridge

Jialing Qiao Lu

St. Lu

Zhong shan

Renmin Lu

People's Assembly Hall, Renmin Guesthouse /CITS ★

Renhe Jie

SHANGQINGSI

Kangfulai

Sinn Lu

CAAC

Qingsi

Zhongshan Lu

Laozhanya Zheng Jie

Hanwei Lu

to Red Crag Village, Jinyun Mt., Painter's Village and Dazu

Guihua yuan Lu

Jialing Xin Lu

Jiankang Lu

Lu

San Lu

Zhongshan Zhi Lu

Zhong shan

Zhong shan Er Lu

▲ Pipa Hill

Pipa Park

Zhongshan Yi

to Fine Arts Institute, Zoo

Chang jiang

Goose Peak

Chongqing Railway Station

Chongqing City Museum

Pipashan Zheng Jie

Nanqu

Lu

Changjiang Bridge

SHANHUBA   ISLE

SOUTH

N

*No. 5 Wharf

No. 3 Wharf
Passenger Ticket Office • • Chaotianmen
                                  Docks

No. 1
Wharf

• No. 9 Wharf

Wujiang Lu

Jiangbei Zheng Jie

Honghui Lu

Xiaheng Jie

Jinsha Datie Jie

Jialing Cableway

Jialing River

Chaotian Lu

Chaodong Lu

Beiqu

Cangbai Lu

Linjiang Lu

Minzu Lu

Lu

Shaanxi Lu

Shaanxi Lu
Liu Xiang

Huayi Lu

Lu

Wusi Lu

Zourong Lu

★ Huixianlou
Restaurant
Yizhishi   and Hotel

★ Luohan
Temple

★ Chungking
Hotel

Dongshuimen
Wharf No. 12

Minsheng Lu

Department   Liberation
Store   • Monument

Lu

Erfu Jie

Lu

★ Chongqing
Guesthouse

Long-distance
Bus Station

Zhonghua Lu

Bayi Lu

Wuyi Lu

Xinhua Lu

Gongyuan Xiang

Jiefang Dong Lu

Wanglongmen Cableway

Xinmin Jie

Minquan Lu

• Xiaodongtian

Weiyuan

Zuoying Jie

• Wanglongmen
Wharf

Heping Lu

• Taipingmen
Wharf

Kaixuan Lu

Zhong xing Lu

Shiba Ti

Houchi Jie

Shoubei Jie

Xi Lu

• Renhewan
Wharf No. 18

(Yangzi) River

Jiefang

• Chuqimen
Wharf

Changjiang

Xin Jie

Hailang Xi

BANK

Holiday Inn
★

to Nanquenwan Park

0   200   400   600 m
0   200   400   600 yards

★ Yangtze
Hotel

© The Guidebook Company Ltd

THE STORY OF THE THREE KINGDOMS   —by Madeleine Lynn

If one wishes to understand China, one must have some familiarity with the history of the Three Kingdoms and with the lore that surrounds it. Above all this is true on the middle and upper Yangtse where it seems every bend in the river leads to another site associated with this epoch and to the stories that have grown around it like the layers of a pearl around its grain of historical fact. If the events seem complicated and the stage crowded with unfamiliar actors, that too is part of China's reality. One might as well seek to know the Greeks without the Trojan War or the English without Shakespeare.

Lyman P Van Slyke, *Yangtse: Nature, History and the River*, 1988.

By AD 150 the Han dynasty (206 BC–AD 220) was already rotting from within, the result of a series of weak emperors. The uprising of peasant rebels known as the Yellow Turbans (AD 184) gave three strong warlords (Cao Cao, Liu Bei and Sun Quan) the opportunity to amass their own independent armies. They gradually set up rival territories within the Empire and fought it out for the control of China. The history of their struggle formed the basis for the 14th-century popular novel *The Romance of the Three Kingdoms*, a compilation of fact and fiction taken from the repertoires of 12 centuries of storytellers. It is a rambling saga of heroism and treachery, of larger-than-life heroes and villains against the backdrop of the dying dynasty. Tales from this era are also the subject of many Chinese operas.

The three kingdoms were:

The Kingdom of Wei: North China, comprising the Yellow River basin; the base of the Qin and Han dynasties. Its ruler was Cao Cao, Duke of Wei, characterized in the novel as the archetypal Chinese villain, a brilliant but ruthless general. 'Speak of Cao Cao and he is there' is the Chinese equivalent of 'Talk of the devil'.

The Kingdom of Shu: the area that is now called Sichuan. It was established by Liu Bei, pretender to the throne by virtue of being a distant relation of the Han emperor. Although a rather weak and insignificant personality himself, his royal blood attracted gifted followers, the most famous of whom are Zhuge Liang and Liu's two sworn blood-brothers Zhang Fei and Guan Yu (*see* page 54).

Zhuge Liang was Liu's premier strategist and has been held up as an example of military genius ever since. There are numerous stories of how he defeated Cao Cao's larger armies by guile and bravado rather than strength. For instance, there was the time he was staying in an unprotected city when Cao Cao's army arrived unexpectedly. As the troops approached, they saw that the city gate was wide open and that Zhuge Liang, accompanied only by one young servant boy, was perched on top of the city wall calmly playing the harp. Convinced that they were about to walk into an ambush, the enemy withdrew.

Guan Yu was so revered for his loyalty that he was gradually turned into a god. Given the honorary title Guan Gong, and also known as Guan Di, God of War, Justice and Righteousness, until recently nearly every large town in China had a temple dedicated to him. His statue can be recognized by its distinctive red face, signifying bravery and goodness.

The Kingdom of Wu: The rich and fertile lower Yangzi region, as far as the sea. This was controlled by the treacherous Sun Quan, whose family was the most influential in the region.

Between Shu and Wu was the middle Yangzi basin, a no-man's land of marshes and lakes. From here one could threaten either Shu or Wu and it was here that some of the most crucial battles took place. On the run from Cao Cao's army, Liu Bei took refuge in this area and Zhuge Liang persuaded Sun Quan, the ruler of Wu, to ally with them against the powerful Cao Cao. Although their combined forces were still far less than Cao Cao's, together they routed him in the critical battle of Red Cliff (see page 93), at a site upriver from modern Wuhan.

Now it was Cao Cao's turn to flee for his life. Although Guan Yu actually cornered him and could have killed him he let him go, as Cao Cao had done the same for him in an earlier encounter.

But the alliance between Liu Bei and Sun Quan did not last long. Sun Quan tried to persuade Guan Yu to betray Liu Bei and join him. When Guan Yu refused, Sun had him beheaded and sent his head to Cao Cao, hoping for an alliance with him. The grief-stricken Liu Bei ignored Zhuge Liang's advice and launched a disastrous campaign against Sun. Before the fight even began, his other sworn brother Zhang Fei was murdered by two fellow officers who planned to surrender to Sun. Liu was ignominiously defeated and retreated to Baidi Cheng, where he died a few years later.

Cao Cao also died without achieving his ambitions. Although his son succeeded in conquering the other two Kingdoms, it was a short-lived triumph, as he was toppled in a *coup d'état*. So none of the three protaganists realized their dream of ruling over the whole of China.

44

■ DAZU BUDDHIST CAVES

For tourists staying more than two days in Chongqing, it is possible to make a trip to see the spectacular Buddhist cave carvings of Dazu County.

'Dazu' can be translated in two ways: as 'Great Plenty' or more mundanely as 'Big Foot'. Locals say that Buddha himself left a huge footprint in a nearby pond, and hence the name. The remoteness of the location has protected the caves and the painted sculptures are in excellent condition. Forty sites have been discovered, with 50,000 carvings in 290 niches and grottoes. Seven sites are open to the public, but those at Beishan and Baodingshan are the most frequently visited. The earliest sculptures date from the Tang dynasty (618–907), when the emperors Xuanzong (reigned 712–56) and Xizong (reigned 873–88) fled to Sichuan as civil war broke out in the north. With them came many monks, painters, sculptors and literati, who transformed Sichuan into a centre of culture. Bas-relief carvings of extraordinary grace and detail continued to be created up to the Ming dynasty (1368–1644). Figures and stories from the Buddhist pantheon dominate—a giant reclining Buddha, 31 metres (100 feet) long; a statue of Avalokitesvara seated on a lotus flower, her 1,007 hands spread out over 88 square metres (950 square feet) of rock. An unusual feature here is the carving of scenes from everyday life executed with tender vividness.

The most comfortable way to get to the caves is obviously to hire a car. Provided there is no major delay on the busy road, the return journey can be

Thousand-armed Guanyin, Dazu Buddhist Caves

hurriedly done in one day. Allow for an overnight stay in Dazu and take the bus from Kangfulai Bus Company on Renmin Lu, about a ten-minute walk west from the Renmin Guesthouse. The 160-kilometre (100-mile) ride over hilly country can take up to six hours, but the bus is reasonably comfortable and air-conditioned.

At Dazu make for the Dazu Guesthouse or the Beishan Hotel which cater to foreigners. Trains leave for Dazu twice a day, taking five hours for the journey. The station is 36 kilometres (22 miles) from Dazu town.

Fuling

The river Wu rises in Guizhou, and at its confluence with the Yangzi, stands the ancient town of Fuling on the south bank. Some 2,000 years ago Fuling was the political centre of the Kingdom of Ba (fourth to second centuries BC) and the site of its ancestral graves.

Fuling is the connecting link in water transportation between northern Guizhou and eastern Sichuan. The town and its surrounding area are rich in such produce as grain, lacquer and tung oil, and the local specialities are hot pickled mustard tuber, Hundred-Flower sweet wine and pressed radish seeds.

West of the town is the White Crane Ridge, on which are carved ancient water level marks in the form of 14 scaled fish, and many inscriptions referring to the hydrology of the river at this point. These stone fish—the oldest of which was carved in the Tang dynasty (618–907)—are visible only at the lowest water level, which occurs perhaps once every decade or so. Locals say that 'when the stone fish appear the harvests will be good'.

In 1972 archaeologists excavated graves from the Kingdom of Ba, and among the finds were ancient musical instruments.

Fengdu

Fengdu, on the north bank of the river, was in the past more popularly known as the 'City of Ghosts'. There is a temple here dedicated to the God of Hades. A pilgrim to the temple used to be able to purchase, for the sum of one dollar, a 'Passport to Heaven', stamped by the local magistrate and the abbot. Landmarks in the town bore horrific names—Ghost Torturing Pass, Last Glance at Home Tower, Nothing-to-be-done Bridge. Fengdu's temples display instruments of torture and wild demon images. Shopkeepers kept a basin of water into which customers threw their coins: if they sank they were genuine, but if they floated the coins were ghost money and unacceptable. Boats would moor in midstream rather than by the bank in case of attack by ghosts. It seems that the origin of the town's extraordinary reputation dates back to the Han dynasty (206 BC–AD 220) when two officials, Yin and Wang, became Daoist (Taoist) recluses here and eventually Immortals. When combined, their names mean 'King of the Underworld'. Today, however, the town is thronged with tourists attracted by temples and shrines dedicated to the gods of the underworld. The ski lift to the original temple complex at Minshan costs 15 *yuan* roundtrip. Otherwise it is a 30-minute hike starting at the Bridge to the Otherworld.

Zhongxian

There are two moving stories about how Zhongxian (Loyal County) got its name. In the Warring States period (475–221 BC), Ba Manzi, a native of Zhongxian, became a general to the army of the Kingdom of Ba. Towards the end of the Zhou dynasty the Kingdom of Ba was in a state of civil war, and Ba Manzi was sent to the Kingdom of Chu to beg military assistance to put down the rebellion. The price demanded by Chu was the forfeit of three Ba cities. Once Chu's troops had helped restore stability to Ba, the King of Chu sent his minister to demand the payoff. Ba Manzi, however, said: 'Though I promised Chu the cities you will take my head in thanks to the King of Chu, for the cities of Ba cannot be given away', whereupon he cut off his own head. Receiving his minister's account, the King of Chu sighed: 'Cities would count as nothing had I loyal ministers like Ba Manzi'. He then ordered that Ba Manzi's head be buried with full honours.

The second tale is of another man of Zhongxian, the valiant general Yan Yan, who served the Minor Han dynasty (AD 221–63). Captured by the Shu general Zhang Fei, he refused to surrender, saying boldly: 'In my country we had a general who cut off his own head but we do not have a general who surrendered'. Enraged, Zhang Fei ordered Yan's beheading. The doomed general remained perfectly calm as he asked simply, 'Why are you so angry? If you want to cut off my head then give the order, but there is no point in getting angry and upsetting yourself'. Zhang Fei was so deeply moved by Yan's loyalty and bravery in the face of death that he personally unbound him, treating him as an honoured soldier.

Traditionally, the thick bamboo hawsers used to haul junks over the rapids were made in this area, as the local bamboo is especially tenacious. Today, bamboo handicrafts are a thriving industry, while the local food speciality is Zhongxian beancurd milk.

Shibaozhai (Precious Stone Fortress)

Shibaozhai represents the first gem of Chinese architecture to be encountered on the downstream journey. From afar, the protruding 220-metre (720-foot) hill on the north bank can appear to resemble a jade seal, and is so named. The creation of the hill is attributed to the goddess Nuwo, who caused a rock slide while she was redecorating the sky after a fierce battle between two warring dukes.

A red pavilion hugs one side of this rock. Its tall yellow entrance gate is decorated with lions and dragons and etched with an inscription inviting the visitor to climb the ladder and ascend into a 'Little Fairyland'. The temple at the top was built during the reign of Emperor Qianlong (1736–96) and access to it was by an iron chain attached to the cliff. A nine-storeyed wooden pavilion was added in 1819 so that monks and visitors to the temple would not have to suffer the discomforts of the chain ascent. In 1956 three more storeys were added. Each floor is dedicated to famous generals of the Three Kingdoms period (AD 220–65), local scholars and renowned Chinese poets.

In front of Ganyu Palace at the top of Jade Seal Hill is the Duck Hole. It is said that as spring turns to summer, if you take a live duck and drop it through the hole, it will quickly reappear swimming in the Yangzi. In the past the monks apparently drew their drinking water from this hole by using a pipe made of bamboo.

The spirit wall in the temple's main hall is constructed of excavated Han-dynasty (206 BC–AD 220) bricks. The hall behind is dedicated on the right to Generals Zhang Fei and Yan Yan (see above and page 42) of the Three Kingdoms, and on the left to General Qin Liangyu (1576–1648) who fought bravely against the Manchu forces. A mural shows the goddess Nuwo repairing the sky. Two side corridors and a back hall display archaeological finds and portraits of local Qing-dynasty officials. Fossils of fish and a tail section of a dinosaur found by the river's edge can also be seen.

In the rear hall are the remains of the Rice Flowing Hole. Legend has it that long ago just enough husked rice would flow up from the small hole each day for the needs of the monks and their guests. One day a greedy monk, thinking he could become rich, chiselled a bigger hole, and the rice flow ceased forever.

Many of the tourist cruise ships dock at **Shibaozhai** for a few hours' visit. For those on scheduled passenger boats, you should disembark at **Xituozhen** on the south bank and transfer to local ferries to cross the river.

Wanxian

About two hours below Shibaozhai the boat reaches Wanxian, which is guarded by two nine-storeyed pagodas for good fortune. The city spreads out on both sides of the river and is known as the Gateway to East Sichuan. It is situated high above the river and the foundations of the buildings are many metres high. Porters vie with each other to carry passengers' luggage up the steep stairways to the city. The winding streets vary in level from 29 to 206 metres (95 to 675 feet), so bicycles are a rare

sight. Wanxian has a number of silk-weaving and spinning factories supported by intense silkworm cultivation—operated on a family basis—which continues year round in Wanxian County. Other light industries include tea, bamboo and cane goods, cotton clothing, leather and Chinese medicines. Paper mills utilizing wheat and rice straw from the countryside disgorge milky waste into the Yangzi, adding to the pollution.

In July 1981 the Yangzi River rose 42 metres (138 feet), flooding much of the lower half of the city for three days.

Of the three major regions affected by the proposed Three Gorges Dam (see page 62), Yichang, Wanxian and Chongqing, Wanxian will lose the most. Two-thirds of the total of 1.2 million people to be relocated live in the Wanxian pre-fecture and the reservoir will inundate two-thirds of the city. Over 900 factories are located below the new waterline. Now that the dam has been given the go-ahead, many have already started moving to higher ground and new roads and buildings are being built further up the mountainside.

HISTORY OF WANXIAN
The city received its present name during the Ming dynasty (1368–1644), and became a foreign Treaty Port in 1902. In 1926 two British gunboats bombarded the city, causing massive fires, when the local warlord took to commandeering foreign vessels for the transport of his troops. Following this incident, a boycott on the loading and unloading of British vessels was enforced for several years. This became known as the Wanxian Incident.

As the halfway city between Yichang and Chongqing, Wanxian was a main port for East Sichuan merchandise (including large quantities of tung oil, used in treating wooden junks). Early travellers commented on the huge number of junks anchored at Wanxian. Junks also used to be built here from cypress wood found in the nearby hills.

WHAT TO SEE IN WANXIAN
The downriver boats from Chongqing usually reach Wanxian in the early evening, and depart in the small hours of the following morning.

This enables the passage of the Three Gorges to be made in daylight. Upstream boats also make a long stop. Passengers rush off the boats, hurrying up the hundreds of steps to the town where every night of the year the famous Wanxian rattan and cane market is held on **Shengli Lu**. Buyers and sellers mingle in a frenzy of bargaining for handmade summer bed mats, fans, hats, straw shoes, furniture and basketry. Small, round, red-trimmed baskets with lids are the most popular item and are well known throughout China. Roadside stalls trade in spicy noodles and cooling, opaque soyabean jelly and fresh fruit.

The red pavilion of Shibaozhai (see page 46–7)

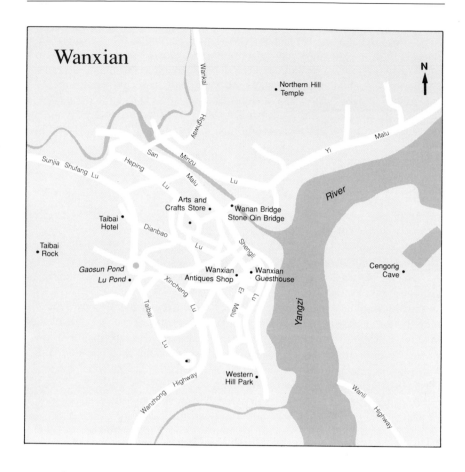

In the mornings, just a little further west of the night market area, one of the city's ten free markets sells local produce and seasonal delicacies such as mountain mushrooms or live eels. **Second Street** (Er Malu) is the main shopping thoroughfare.

There was a community of foreign missionaries in Sichuan before 1949, and two churches—one Catholic and one Protestant—continue to draw sizeable congregations of country folk.

In 1983 a small workshop was set up, employing two teenage boys and a few part-time workers to paint and varnish river stones from the Three Gorges and from the Daning River's Three Little Gorges. These make attractive mementoes and can be bought at the **Arts and Crafts Store**, 1 Third Street (San Malu).

Visitors may also visit silk-weaving and cane-furniture factories.

■ LU POND AND XISHANPAI PAVILION
This small pool, originally dug by a locally revered Song-dynasty official, Lu
Youkai, was once a very large lotus pond surrounded by decorative pavilions.
Now it is not much more than a traffic roundabout. Nearby stands an ancient two-
storey, yellow-tiled pavilion which houses a huge rock carved by the calligrapher
Huang Tingzhen. Around the Xishanpai Pavilion once flowed a winding freshwater channel. Local literati would spend their evenings here, floating full wine
cups along the channel. When a wine cup stopped in front of one of them his
forfeit would be to compose a poem.

■ WESTERN HILL PARK
A clock tower, which dominates the town's skyline from the river, was built in
this large park in 1924. The upper part was damaged by Japanese bombs in 1939.
There is a memorial to a Russian volunteer pilot whose plane crashed in the river
in the same year. During the summer, people relax in bamboo deck-chairs under
the leafy trees, sipping tea and listening to Sichuan-style opera.

■ STONE QIN BRIDGE
A natural bridge in the shape of a Chinese zither crosses Chu River, which di-
vides the town. It is said that Lu Ban, the patron saint of carpenters, spent a
whole night building it.

■ TAIBAI ROCK
The poet Li Bai (701–62) lived here for a time; in the Ming dynasty a memorial
hall was built to commemorate him. Stone inscriptions dating back to the Tang
Dynasty are still to be seen.

■ THE THREE GORGES MUSEUM, WANGZHONG HIGHWAY
This small museum opened in 1994 as a repository of some of the artefacts collected in advance of the flooding of the area by the new dam. Han tomb effigies
and a Ba period 'hanging' coffin are featured. The museum's exhibits are rudi-
mentary, but the shop is extensive—the usual tourist trap with no local products.

Yunyang

The county town of Yunyang (Clouded Sun) is situated on the north bank, 64
kilometres (40 miles) below Wanxian. Opposite, on the south bank, is the handsome Zhang Fei Temple.
   The Tang-dynasty poet, Du Fu (712–70), banished to a minor position in
Sichuan, fell ill while travelling through Yunyang and stayed for many months,
recuperating and writing poetry.

*(following pages) GEOPIC™ image of the Yangzi, taken in 1975 near Wanxian
in eastern Sichuan, just upriver from the Three Gorges*

Yunyang

■ ZHANG FEI TEMPLE

Zhang Fei, the 'Tiger General' of the State of Shu during the Three Kingdoms period (AD 220–65), is revered as a man who kept his word (*see* page 42). In 221, Guan Yu, Zhang Fei's sworn brother, was killed by the armies of the State of Wu. The Tiger General, then an official in Langzhong County, swore revenge and prepared to attack Wu with his army arrayed in white armour and pennants—white being the colour of mourning. He ordered Commanders Zhang Da and Fan Jiang to lead the attack and avenge his brother, under pain of death.

The two pusillanimous officers got Zhang Fei drunk and cut off his head. They then fled by boat to Yunyang, intending to surrender to Wu. Here, however, they heard of a peace settlement between Wu and Shu, and threw Zhang Fei's head into the river, where it circled a fisherman's boat. Zhang Fei appealed to the fisherman in a dream to rescue his head and bury it in Shu. The fisherman obeyed, and the head was interred on Flying Phoenix Hill. A temple was built to commemorate the bold warrior.

It is said that, before internment, the head was placed in a vat of oil, and when copper cash was thrown into the vat, the head would float up to give advice to the lovelorn and childless.

The temple was partly damaged in the flood of 1870, so most of the present ensemble of buildings dates from the late 19th century. It has been extensively restored in the last few years. Sixty per cent of the temple's rich collections of paintings, tablets and inscriptions were lost during the Cultural Revolution. In front of the main hall are giant statues of the three famous sworn blood brothers—Liu Bei, Guan Yu and Zhang Fei. Inside the hall sits the wild-eyed, red-faced Guan Yu; on either side are scenes from his life. The Helpful Wind Pavilion contains steles and huge portraits of the general and his wife. It is said that his spirit, in the form of a helpful wind, frequently assisted passing boats. Junkmen used to stop at the temple to light firecrackers and burn incense in appreciation.

The temple stands amid tranquil gardens, waterfalls and pools.

Fengjie

Fengjie stands on the north bank, just above the western entrance to Qutang, the first of the three great Yangzi gorges. Fengjie town, the county seat for the area, has a population of 50,000. It is an attractive town, with part of its Ming-dynasty city wall intact. The stairways from the ferry pontoons lead up through three old city gates. The town is very lively, thronged with Chinese tourists who have come to visit the famous historical site of Baidi Cheng nearby.

Tourist boats normally stop here for about 20 minutes, which is long enough to enable ongoing passengers to take a brief stroll about the town. Some of the tourist cruise boats make a few hours' stop to allow a visit to Baidi Cheng (*see* page 56); but those on scheduled passenger ships who wish to see Baidi Cheng will have to spend a night at Fengjie.

HISTORY OF FENGJIE

The ancient town was called Kuifu in the Spring and Autumn period (770–476 BC), but became known as Fengjie after the Tang dynasty (618–907). It has long been famous as a poets' city, as many of China's greatest poets commemorated their visits here with verses. The Tang-dynasty poet Du Fu (712–70) wrote some 430 poems while serving as an official here for two years.

Liu Bei, the King of Shu during the Three Kingdoms period (AD 220–65, *see* page 42), died of despair in the Eternal Peace Palace after he was defeated by the armies of Wu. According to two ancient tablets unearthed in recent years, the Fengjie Teacher Training Institute now stands on the site of the palace. On his deathbed, Liu Bei entrusted his sons to the care of his loyal adviser, Zhuge Liang, entreating him to educate them in wisdom and to choose the most talented one to succeed him as king.

It was here that Zhuge Liang trained the troops of Shu in military strategy. He constructed the Eight Battle Arrays, 64 piles of stones 1.5 metre (5-foot) high erected in a grid pattern, 24 of which represented the surrounding troops. The principles of Zhuge Liang's manoeuvres have long been studied by China's military strategists and continue to be relevant to present-day concepts of Chinese warfare.

Nearby is the village of **Yufu**, which means 'the fish turns back' and relates to the legend of Qu Yuan, China's famous poet and statesman of the third century BC. During his service at court, the country was riven by factions and discord. His political enemies had him exiled; eventually, in despair, he drowned himself in Dongting Lake. His body was allegedly swallowed by a sacred fish which then swam up the gorges to Qu Yuan's birthplace, near Zigui (*see* page 76), where the fish intended to give Qu Yuan an honourable burial. However, so great were the lamentations and weeping of the mourners along the shore that the fish also became tearful and swam past Zigui. It was not until it reached Yufu that the fish realized its mistake and turned back.

WHAT TO SEE IN FENGJIE

Fengjie is typical of many of the Yangzi River towns. Its markets on **Zhonghua Lu**, **Heping Lu** and **Fandi Lu** are filled with local produce, clothing and Chinese mountain herbs. Its fruits—especially peaches, pomelos and snow-pears—are famous. Yellow-poplar combs were a speciality, but are now rare. **Dadongmen Jie** is lined with leafy trees and traditional whitewashed two-storeyed houses—the upper storey frequently in wood—and was once called Zhuge Liang Jie (*see* page 42), for it is said he passed this way. Outside the city wall, above the river, are makeshift mat-shed tea-houses where the local men and travellers relax in bamboo deck-chairs, drinking tea and eating sunflower seeds or eggs boiled in tea. When summer floods threaten, these temporary sheds are simply dismantled and re-erected once the water subsides.

Baidi Cheng (White Emperor City)

The local ferry from Fengjie takes about 20 minutes to reach Baidi Cheng on the north bank of the river, passing several pagodas on the surrounding peaks (the return trip takes an hour). Sadly the approach to this historic site is quite spoilt by a factory and workers' housing built in the 1970s.

Because of its strategic position the town was chosen in the first century by Gong Sunshu, an official turned soldier, as the site of his headquarters. The legend goes that in AD 25 white vapour in the shape of a dragon was seen rising from a nearby well. Taking this as an auspicious omen, Gong declared himself the 'White Emperor' and the town 'White Emperor City'. Remains of the city wall can still be seen on the hill behind Baidi Mountain. The 12-year reign of the White Emperor was regarded as a time of peace and harmony, so after his death a temple was built to commemorate his reign. This temple dates back over 1,950 years.

Several hundred steps lead up the wooded Baidi Mountain. **The Western Pavilion** (at one time known as Guanyin Dong) on the slope is believed to have been occupied by the great poet Du Fu, who wrote numerous poems at this site. The pavilion overlooks what Du Fu described as 'the limitless Yangzi'. Further up the hill is a *stupa*, marking the grave of a much-loved literary monk who served at the temple during the Qing dynasty (1644–1911).

A red wall with an imposing yellow dragon-head gateway surrounds the temple complex. Though the temple was originally dedicated to Gong Sunshu, the White Emperor, his statue was removed in the Ming dynasty (1368–1644) and replaced with images of Liu Bei, Zhuge Liang, Guan Yu and Zhang Fei, heroes of the Shu Kingdom during the Three Kingdoms period (see page 42). The present halls date from the Ming dynasty.

The front hall contains large modern statues which depict Liu Bei on his deathbed entrusting his sons to the care of Zhuge Liang (see page 55). To the left is the handsome, winged **Observing the Stars Pavilion (Guanxing Ting)**, where a large bronze bell can be seen hanging in the upper storey. From this pavilion Zhuge Liang observed the stars and made accurate weather forecasts which helped him plan his victorious battles. The two Forest of Tablets halls contain several rare engraved stelae, some of which are over 1,300 years old. The Phoenix Tablet is particularly finely engraved. The Bamboo Leaf Poem Tablet is one of only three in China. It is

Tiger Leaping Gorge on the upper reaches of the Yangzi River in Yunnan Province

considered a fine work of art, combining as it does poetry and calligraphy, for the tablet is engraved with three branches of bamboo, each leaf forming the Chinese characters of a poem.

The **Wuhou Hall** is dedicated to Zhuge Liang, his son and grandson. The bodies of the statues are of the Ming dynasty (1368–1644), but the heads, smashed in the Cultural Revolution (1966–76), are new. **Mingliang Hall** is dedicated to Liu Bei, who is shown surrounded by four attendants, as well as the black-faced Zhang Fei and the red-faced Guan Yu on one side, and Zhuge Liang on the other. Adjoining rooms display furniture, scrolls, porcelain and other cultural relics.

In 1987, several buildings were converted to form a museum displaying the many cultural relics found within the area, including two coffins from the Ba culture. One of these dates back to the Western Han dynasty (206 BC–AD 8).

Fine views of the entrance to **Qutang Gorge** can be seen from the temple. When the proposed Three Gorges Dam (*see* page 62) is built further downriver in the Xiling Gorge, near Yichang, the water level will rise and Baidi Mountain will become an island.

At the foot of Baidi Mountain, the **Yanyu Rock**—over 30 metres (100 feet) long, 20 metres (66 feet) wide and 40 metres (130 feet) high—used to be a

The Yangzi Gorges

constant hazard to boats riding the swift current and heading into the narrow
entrance of Qutang Gorge. Over the ages, countless vessels perished. In 1959 it
took a work team seven days to blow up this gigantic rock.

Qutang Gorge

Immediately below Baidi City is **Kui Men**, the entrance to the first of the three
gorges of the Yangzi River—the eight-kilometre (five-mile) long Qutang Gorge
(also known by early Western travellers as the Wind Box Gorge). The shortest
but grandest of them all, the gorge's widest point is only 150 metres (500 feet).
Mists frequently swirl around the mysterious limestone peaks, some nearly 1,200
metres (4,000 feet) high, and the river rushes swift as an arrow through the narrow entrance, pounding the perpendicular cliff faces on either side of the gorge.

This gorge was a particularly dangerous stretch during high-water seasons and
has been known to rise to 50 metres (165 feet). An upper Yangzi steamboat captain
recalled how in September 1929 the level of water was 75 metres (246 feet), and

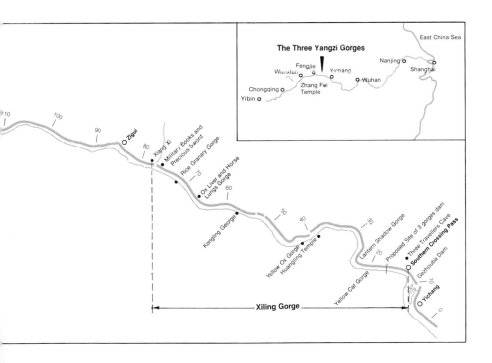

likened the passage to a trough, with the water banked up on both sides. His ship became quite unmanageable, and was carried down, broadside on, only coming under control again at the lower end. He would never, he vowed, try to negotiate it again at such a level.

Two mountains—the **Red Passage Mountain (Chijia Shan)** to the north, once compared to a celestial peach, and the **White Salt Mountain (Baiyan Shan)** to the south—form the Kui Men entrance, their steep precipices like the wings of a giant door guarding the tumultuous waters.

In the Tang dynasty (618–907) chains were strung across the river as an 'iron lock' to prevent passage of enemy boats. In the Song dynasty (960–1279) two iron pillars nearly two metres (six feet) tall were erected on the north side, and seven chains, some 250 metres (820 feet) long, were used to block the river passage. Although the original purpose was defensive, the chain locks were later used to enable local authorities to gather taxes from all boats travelling downriver. This system continued until the middle Qing dynasty (1644–1911). The iron pillars are only visible at low water.

On the precipice of White Salt Mountain (south side) are a series of holes nearly a metre (three feet) apart and about one-third of a metre (one foot) deep, forming a 'Z' shape. These are known as the **Meng Liang Stairway**. According to legend, Yang Jiye, a Song-dynasty general, was buried on a terrace high up on the mountain. His loyal comrade-in-arms, Meng Liang, decided secretly to take the bones back for burial in Yang's home town. In the dead of night he took a small boat into the gorge and began to hack out a pathway to the terrace. Halfway up the rock face he was discovered by a monk who began crowing like a cock. Meng Liang, thinking that dawn was breaking and fearing discovery, abandoned his task. When he later discovered the monk's mischief, he was so provoked that he hung the monk upside down over a precipice. The rock below Meng Liang Stairway is known as **Hanging Monk Rock (Daodiao Heshangshi)**. History records, however, that General Yang was not buried here and the steps are probably the remains of an ancient river pathway. Sections of a city wall, 1,400 years old, have been found on top of White Salt Mountain, so it is possible that the pathway led to this early settlement. Another theory about the stairway suggests that it was built to provide access to the rare medicinal herbs which grow high on the cliff faces.

At the highest point above Hanging Monk Rock one can see **Armour Cave (Kuang-jia Dong)** where it is said a Song-dynasty woman general hid her weapons. In 1958 the cave was explored and found to contain three 2,000-year old wooden coffins from the Kingdom of Ba, in which were bronze swords and lacquered wooden combs.

Near the Meng Liang Stairway is the **Drinking Phoenix Spring**, a stalagmite in the shape of a phoenix drinking the sweet spring-water. Nearby is the **Chalk Wall**

The Three Gorges Dam —by Madeleine Lynn

The dream of a dam to tame the treacherous Three Gorges and harness the energy of the Yangzi has been around since 1919, when Sun Yatsen first proposed it in his ambitious blueprint, 'Grand Tactics to Build up the Country'. But the project has been dogged by delays and controversy ever since. Detailed surveys undertaken in the 1930s and 1940s came to nothing because of the war. Although Chairman Mao gave it his blessing in the 1950s, the ensuing debate was so fierce that it was agreed to conduct another 15–20 years of research. It was finally approved in 1992. Work began in 1993 and is scheduled to be completed in 2010. However, there is still strong opposition to the project and the high cost, technical difficulties and environmental concerns make many people doubt if it will ever be completed.

The statistics are staggering. It is planned to be by far the largest hydro-electric project in the world, with a capacity of 17,680 megawatts of electricity. The largest output at present is 10,300 megawatts, from the Guri Dam in Venezuela. The Three Gorges Dam will submerge 570,000 acres of farmland and the homes of an estimated 1.2 to 1.3 million people, the largest population ever to be relocated for such a project. Most of them will be moved to higher ground in the same area, although some may migrate to the coastal provinces, where there are labour shortages.

The dam site is 44 kilometres (27 miles) upstream from Yichang city proper, at Sandouping Village, inside the first of the Three Gorges. It will turn the stretch of river from Sandouping to Chongqing into a reservoir 600 kilometres (370 miles) long. Thus nearly the whole length of the Three Gorges, with their magnificent scenery, historical sites and legends, will be dramatically changed.

Meanwhile the debate continues. Those in favour of the dam have three main arguments: first and most important, it will help control the frequent floods, such as the one in 1954, which killed 33,000 people. The last major flood was in 1981. Even in a normal year, the water level can vary by as much as 30 metres (98 feet) between the dry and wet seasons. The argument runs that when the dam is built, the water flow can be controlled and released gradually, and thus floods in the lower reaches below the dam can be alleviated. In some parts of the lower reaches the Yangzi is a 'hanging river', with the water level higher than the towns nestled behind their dikes. If these dikes should burst, thousands could drown. The city of Shashi for instance, lies 3–7 metres (10–23 feet) below the level of the water in high season. There is a popular saying: 'Inside your house you raise your eyes, above your head the boat passes by.'

Second, the dam would provide much-needed electricity and third, by submerging the dangerous rocks and reefs, the Gorges will be both safer and easier to navigate.

Those against the dam argue that it will be an environmental disaster, built more to gratify China's leaders' desire for a monument than for sound engineering reasons. Not everyone agrees that the dam will make a significant difference to flooding in the lower reaches. Many experts claim that the water behind the dam will silt up, creating a huge, muddy quagmire. Thus some calculate that within 80 years of the dam being built, shipping could come to a halt. The Yangzi carries 523 million tons of sediment a year, and is already subject to siltage. The dam will slow down the water, which will increase siltage and also pollution, as the garbage and factory effluents discharged into the river will not disperse as fast. Some claim that the vast reservoir will also increase the amount of cloud in Chongqing in particular, a city already notorious for its perpetual haze. Chongqing's polluted air produces fog with a high acid content, so residents' health will suffer.

Then there is the Baiji river dolphin, already extinct in other habitats, and on the Chinese government's endangered species list. Their chances of survival are very precarious even without the dam, but the environmental changes that it will bring could be the final death blow.

Cost is another concern. Critics argue that the official estimate of 121 billion yuan (US$15 billion) does not take into account inflation and cost overruns and point to the Gezhouba Dam, which ended up costing more than three times the original estimate. In addition, they point out that the dam makes a tempting military target.

However, the Chinese government seems determined to press ahead. Construction has begun on the preliminary coffer-dam and from Yichang to Chongqing, factories and farmers alike are moving to higher ground. For some, particularly young city dwellers, the dam promises a better life: more modern housing and perhaps a job in a new factory. For others, however, it means leaving the land their families have tilled for generations and moving to less fertile ground.

Tracking through the Rapids

Though the junk was now apparently safe, for it breasted the smooth, swift water of the second sluice and was no longer being thrown from side to side, the heaviest work still remained to be done. I turned to watch the trackers, for theirs was now the heavy work of making many tons of cypress go uphill on a fiercely resisting roadway of water. It was a moving sight—horribly depressing, to see more than three hundred human beings reduced to the level of work animals, blind-folded asses and oxen; yet thrilling too, to see the irresistible force of their co-operation, for the three hundred and fifty cloth shoes of their each step up the slope were planted in the same moment, and the sad trackers' cries, 'Ayah! . . . Ayah!,' were sung in a great unison choir of agony and joy, and the junk did move.

It moved, however, more and more slowly, as the last and hardest test of the trackers' labor began—heaving the junk over the head of the rapid, over the round, swift crest of the sluice. The bow of the junk seemed to dig into the water there. The rope grew taut. The great crowd of towing men hung for a long time unable to move. I saw the cook look down toward the junk, obviously at a loss what to do.

Then suddenly from midstream, from the very center of danger, came a lovely, clear, high-pitched line of song.

It was Old Pebble. I looked out and saw him standing on the deck, himself leaning as if to pull, hurling a beautiful song at the crowd on the bank.

On the proper beat the many trackers gave out a kind of growl and moved their feet forward a few inches, and the bow of the junk dug deeper into the head of the sluice. They took a second, firmer step. And a third, and a fourth.

I had never heard Old Pebble sing such a haunting melody. I saw that he was in a kind of ecstasy. His face shone in a grimace of hard work and happiness. I remembered my doubts about his credo of 'simplicity', which he had recited to me in our first evening on the river, and I remembered my distress that such a sturdy young man did not avow personal goals of wealth, love, honor, and fame. Now I saw from his face that this was his life's goal; this instant of work, this moment's line of song, this accord with his poor fellow men, this brief spurt of useful loyalty to the cranky, skinny, half-mad owner of the junk on which he had shipped, and above all this fleeting triumph over the Great River.

At last the junk raised its head, shivered, and shot suddenly forward into the still water of the pond above the rapids.

When it was over, and the junk was pulled up to the loading platform, Old Pebble was streaming sweat, but he looked very happy.

I walked down to the river's edge to see what he would say. He jumped ashore and bent down to the river and scooped up double handfuls of the brown water and washed his face, sloshing and snorting like a small boy. I moved near him. He looked up. All he said was, 'Ayah, this river is a turtle.'

John Hersey, A Single Pebble, 1914

(Fengbi Tang) where 900 characters, dating from the Song dynasty, have been carved by famous calligraphers on the rock face. The site derives its name from the limestone powder which was used to smooth rock surfaces before being carved.

On the north side of the river, opposite Meng Liang Stairway, is a coffee-coloured precipice called **Bellows Gorge (Fengxiang Xia)**. The name refers to some square configurations in the rock face, which were supposed to be bellows used by Lu Ban, the god of carpenters. In 1971 the secret of Bellows Gorge was revealed, when ancient suspended wooden coffins, similar to those found in the Armour Cave, were discovered in the caves of the precipice. Some of these have been moved to museums, but three remain and can be seen from the river.

Wise Grandmother's Spring (Shenglao Quan) in a rock crevice on the southern bank was, according to legend, created by an immortal grandmother from heaven for thirsty travellers. They had only to call out to the spring 'Worthy Grandmother, a drink!' and water would gush for a moment from the rock.

East of Armour Cave (on the south side), on the top of a black rock, is a huge stone which the Chinese say resembles the body of a rhinoceros looking westwards as if forever enjoying 'the autumn moon over the gorge gate'. They call this rock **Rhinoceros Looking at the Moon**.

From Baidi Cheng to Daixi through the whole length of Qutang Gorge, visitors may see, high up on the northern face, the old towpath, hand-hewn in 1889 by the local people. Prior to this there existed a smaller towpath which was often submerged at high water. Remnants of this path can still be seen below Bellows Gorge. Travellers had to abandon their boats and climb over the peaks, a dangerous and time-wasting detour. Boats going upstream had to wait for a favourable east wind; if the wind was in the wrong quarter, boats could be stranded in the water for ten days or more.

The sandstone walls of the gorges have become pitted by natural erosion, causing lines of holes, some of which are several metres deep. The town of **Daixi**, at the mouth of a stream bearing the same name, marks the eastern end of Qutang Gorge. Over 200 burial sites have been found here, and excavations have revealed a rich collection of bone, stone and jade artifacts and pottery, as well as various burial forms of the middle and late New Stone Age period.

Below Daixi the river widens out. About five kilometres (three miles) downstream, on the south bank, are two sharp, black peaks which form the **Unlocked Gates Gorge (Suokai Xia)**. On the west side of the gorge, midway up the mountain, is a semi-circular stone shaped roughly like a drum—this is the **Beheading Dragon Platform (Zhanglong Tai)**. Facing this on the opposite side of the gorge is a thick, round stone pillar, the **Binding Dragon Pillar (Suolong Zhu)**. Once upon a time, the Jade Dragon, a son of the Dragon of the Eastern Sea, lived in a cave on the upper reaches of the Daixi Stream. One season he decided to visit his family by way of the Yangzi, but shortly afterwards found himself lost. Changing into the form of an old man, he asked his way of a herds boy. The boy pointed north with his sickle. The dragon rushed off in that direction but again got lost, whereupon he flew into a mighty rage and rushed at the mountains, causing them to crumble and dam up the river; farmlands were flooded, earthquakes toppled houses, and men and animals perished. At this moment the Goddess Yao Ji rushed to the spot on a cloud. She rebuked Jade Dragon, but he was unrepentant. She flung a string of pearls into the air; it changed into a rope that bound the dragon to the stone pillar. Yao Ji then ordered the great Da Yu, controller of rivers, to behead the murderous dragon on the nearby platform. He then diverted the river by cutting the gorge. The people of this valley have lived happily ever since.

Two kilometres (1.2 miles) further, the Baozi Tan (a triple rapid) and the Xiama Tan used to be serious dangers to shipping at low-water level. A traveller on one of the Yangzi steamships in the 1930s remarked:

> Only the throbbing of the engines as the bow entered the most turbulent part of the rapid, and buried its nose deep in the boiling water, revealed its presence to the uninitiated. But on looking back one could see that there had been a drop of two or three feet in the water where the rapid was most violent. Above it was a series of whirlpools and races.

Wushan

Wushan County is situated above the Yangzi on the north bank and embraced by lovely mountain peaks where flourishes the tung tree, whose oil was used for the caulking, oiling and varnishing of junks and sampans. The small town of Wuxia, with 15,000 residents, is the county seat. Wuxia is the starting point for boat trips up the Daning River through the Three Little Gorges—the main reason for making a stop at Wushan.

HISTORY OF WUSHAN
The town has existed since the latter part of the Shang dynasty (c. 1600–1027 BC). In the Warring States period (475–221 BC), the King of Chu established a palace west of the city. During the first century, the faith of the Buddha had reached China and many temples were built here; almost all the temples have been destroyed over the years. The name of the town originates with Wu Xian, a successful Tang-dynasty doctor to the imperial court, who was buried on Nanling Mountain, on the south

bank opposite Wushan. A winding path—with 108 bends—leads from the foot of the mountain to the summit where there is a small temple. This path was an official road through to Hubei Province in ancient times.

WHAT TO SEE IN WUSHAN
The streets of this long and narrow town are named after the 12 peaks of the Wu Gorge. The old houses are mostly two-storeyed, with central courtyards on whose walls hang baskets of dried medicinal herbs. The markets supply the essentials for mountain living—back-baskets, broad-brimmed woven hats with plastic or waxed paper crowns to keep off the frequent summer rains, plastic and straw sandals (best for coping with the slippery mud after rain) and agricultural tools. Several street dentists with pedal-driven drills await customers. Some householders still use traditional stone grinders and pounders to make their wheat- and rice-flour. There is a fine old Chinese medicine shop at **38 Songluan Jie**. Although there is little left of the many temples here, one may visit, weather permitting, **Gaoqiu Mountain**, to the northwest of the town. This was the site of the King of Chu's palace and of Gaotang Temple, built to commemorate the fairy goddess Yao Ji and Emperor Da Yu, Controller of Rivers. According to the Daoist (Taoist) legend, it was on this site that Da Yu camped while cutting the three Yangzi River Gorges.

The energetic visitor may climb to the summit of Wushan (Witches Hill), a two-hour hike. Worshippers still come to a small shrine here, built within the ruins of an old Buddhist monastery. From the summit the views of Wu Gorge and the river are spectacular. A less strenuous outing may be made to the newly opened limestone cave complex in Wu Gorge high up on the cliff face above the south bank of the river. This involves a short boat ride from Wushan town, an easy scramble up the rocky slope and then a walk along the old towpath. Around the cave complex there are the usual teahouse and ornamental pavilions. The cave complex, Luyou Dong, is named after a Song-dynasty official who visited Wushan and left an appreciative record of his stay.

DANING RIVER EXCURSION: THE THREE LITTLE GORGES
This breathtakingly beautiful area has only been open to foreign tourism since 1985 and for this reason it remains largely unspoilt. A day trip up the crystal-clear Daning River through its magnificent Three Little Gorges (Xiao Sanxia)—whose total length is only 33 kilometres (20 miles)—is to experience the excitement and awe of bygone days of river travel in China.

The excursion is undertaken in long, low, wooden motorized *sampans*, whose strong experienced boatmen pole with all their might when the river is too shallow for the engine to be used, heaving their bodies forward as they thrust long iron-

One of the Lesser Three Gorges

Cool Depths

Stars and Moon on the Yangtse

After sudden rain, a clear autumn night.
On golden waves the sparkle of the Jewelled Cord.
The River of Heaven white from eternity,
The Yangtse's shallows limpid since just now.
Reflections, pearls from a snapped string:
High in the sky one mirror rises.
Afterlight which fades as the clock drips,
Still fainter as the dewdrops settle on the flowers.

Du Fu (712–770),
translated by A C Graham

Sadness of the Gorges

Above the gorges, one thread of sky:
Cascades in the gorges twine a thousand cords.
High up, the slant of splintered sunlight, moonlight:
Beneath, curbs to the wild heave of the waves.
The shock of a gleam, and then another,
In depths of shadow frozen for centuries:
The rays between the gorges do not halt at noon;
Where the straits are perilous, more hungry spittle.
Trees lock their roots in rotted coffins
And the twisted skeletons hang tilted upright:
Branches weep as the frost perches
Mournful cadences, remote and clear.
A spurned exile's shrivelled guts
Scald and seethe in the water and fire he walks through.
A lifetime's like a fine-spun thread,
The road goes up by the rope at the edge.
When he pours his libation of tears to the ghosts in the stream
The ghosts gather, a shimmer on the waves.

Meng Jiao (751–814),
translated by A C Graham

tipped bamboo poles into the riverbed, and following through until they are almost lying on their backs in their struggle against the current. Few of the local boats encountered are motorized and the boatmen must tow the boats— laden with local merchandise and coal—upriver, using a long bamboo rope and tracking in harness, along the water's edge or along cut pathways in the rock face, chanting as they go. Negotiating a rapid may take several exhausting attempts before the boat is finally hauled over.

About 40 minutes from the mouth of the river, at its confluence with the Yangzi, the entrance to the first of the gorges is reached. This is the **Dragon Gate Gorge (Longmen Xia)**, three kilometres (1.8 miles) long. On the cliff face to the right is the 1981 flood mark, over 40 metres (130 feet) above river level. The mouth of the gorge is like a massive gateway through which the river rushes like a green dragon, hence its name. The gateway appears to shut once one has passed through. On the east side is **Dragon Gate Spring (Longmen Quan)** and above it **Lingzhi Peak**, topped by the **Nine-Dragon Pillar**. On this peak, it is said, grow strange plants and the fungus of longevity (*lingzhi*), guarded by nine dragons. On the western bank, two rows of 15-centimetre (2-inch) square holes, continuing the entire length of the small gorges and numbering over 6,000 are all that remain of an astonishing plank walkway, which was first constructed in the Han period and recorded in the Annals of Wushan County in 246 BC. Wooden stakes inserted into these hand-hewn holes supported planks and large bamboo pipes, which stretched for 100 kilometres (62 miles) along the river. This pipeline conveyed brine, while the planks provided an access for maintenance. In the 17th century the pathway, used by the peasant leader Li Zicheng in his uprising against the Ming dynasty, was destroyed by the imperial army.

After leaving the gorge the boat passes the **Nest of Silver Rapid (Yinwo Tan)**. In the past, rich merchants trading in the hinterland often came to grief here; perhaps there are caches of silver under the bubbling surface still! In 1958 work began on clearing major obstacles from the river.

The Daning then meanders through terraced hillsides before entering the 10-kilometre (6-mile) **Misty Gorge (Bawu Xia)**, with its dramatic scenery of rocks, peaks and caves, including Fairy Maiden Cave, Fairy Throwing a Silk Ball, and Guanyin Seated on a Lotus Platform. A long, layered formation, like a scaly dragon, can be seen on the eastern cliff. Suspended upon the precipice is a relic of the ancient inhabitants of eastern Sichuan 2,000 years ago, an 'iron' coffin (which is actually made of wood that has turned black with age). This gorge is accordingly also known as **Iron Coffin Gorge**.

The village of **Twin Dragons** or **Shuanglong** (population 300), above Bawu Gorge, is the halfway point. Lunch is provided at the reception centre, which also has ten rooms for overnight accommodation.

Emerald Green Gorge (Dicui Xia), 20 kilometres (12.5 miles) long, is inhabited by wild ducks and covered with luxuriant bamboo groves from which rises a deafening cacophany of bird-song. There are also many types of monkey still to be seen if you are lucky. Once their shrill cries resounded throughout the Yangzi gorges, but today they can be heard only in Dicui Gorge. River stones of an extraordinary variety and colour can be gathered. These are painted and sold as artistic souvenirs in Wanxian (*see* page 50).

At the end of this gorge the tourist boat turns around and rushes downstream, arriving at Wushan in half the time it took to get here, aided by the skilful use of the long *yuloh*, which is weighted by a stone to steady the boat.

Groups may hire a boat for this trip at the mouth of the Daning River. Cheap local ferries also do this trip but it takes much longer and requires an overnight stop at Dachang (a town with fine farmhouse architecture and the remains of a Qing-dynasty city gate); to do this you must be accompanied by an official from Wushan.

Wu Xia (Witches Gorge)

Below Wushan the river approaches the entrance to the 40-kilometre (25-mile) long Wu Gorge, the middle Yangzi gorge which straddles Sichuan and Hubei Provinces. So sheer are the cliffs that it is said the sun rarely penetrates. The boat passes, on the south side, the **Golden Helmet and Silver Armour Gorge (Jinkuang Yinjia Xia)** shaped, it is said, like an ancient warrior's silver coat of arms crowned by a round golden helmet. Ahead are the 12 peaks of Wu Gorge, famed for their dark and sombre grace. Poets have attempted to evoke both their bleakness and beauty:

Autumn Thoughts
Jade dews deeply wilt and wound the maple woods;
On Witch Mountain, in Witch Gorge, the air is sombre, desolate.
Billowy waves from the river roar and rush towards the sky
Over the frontier pass, wind and clouds sink to the darkening earth.
These clustered chrysanthemums, twice blooming, evoke the tears of yesteryear,
A lonely boat, as ever, is moored to the heart that yearns for home.
To cut winter clothes, women everywhere ply their scissors and foot-rulers
Below the White Emperor's tall city is heard the urgent pounding of the evening wash.

Six peaks line the north side:
Climbing Dragon Peak (Denglong Feng)

How Much for a Life?

In 1854, a rich merchant living near Xin Tan, one of the most dangerous of all the rapids in the Three Gorges, raised subscriptions to build three life-boats. Painted red to distinguish them from regular craft, they soon became known as the Red Boats. More money was raised over the years to increase the fleet and in the 1880s the running of the service was taken over by the government, although funds still came from public subscription. By the early 1900s there were almost 50 boats stationed along the river. In 1899 alone they saved 1,473 lives from 49 wrecked junks.

A Red Boat would accompany each vessel on the most perilous parts of the journey—being dragged upstream by the trackers over the different sets of rapids. Downstream voyages were not as dangerous, so a special escort was not deemed necessary. When a wreck occurred a gun was fired as the summons for all Red Boats to come and help.

The life boats were not allowed to salvage cargo from the wrecks. However, there was a reward system for the salvaging of human beings. W E Geil, who travelled along the Yangzi in 1904 on his way to Burma, describes how it worked:

On life-saving the Chinese have curious notions. While eating cakes cooked in lamp oil in a tea house in Chintan village, the skipper of the Red Boat came in and I asked him certain questions about the pagoda for destitute souls. He told me that for the recovery of a dead body from the water, a reward of eight hundred cash is given by the Emperor. It used to be eight hundred cash for saving a live man and four hundred for a dead one. But it was soon discovered that this did not pay, so it was reversed, and now four hundred cash are given to save a live man and eight hundred to recover a dead one. This allows four hundred cash to bury the man if he dies after being taken out of the water. This interesting fact was further explained to me by another of the Red Boat men—that the dead man involves funeral expenses and the live man none! This is good Celestial reasoning. It would be more profitable to drown a man before pulling him out. I found out afterwards that the reward of four hundred cash is given provided the rescuer gets his clothes wet; otherwise he gets but two hundred.

W E Geil, A Yankee on the Yangtse, 1904

Sage Spring Peak (Shengquan Feng)
Facing Clouds Peak (Chaoyun Feng)
Goddess Peak (Shennu Feng)
Fir Tree Cone Peak (Songluan Feng)
Congregated Immortals Peak (Jixian Feng)

Three peaks flank the south side:
Assembled Cranes Peak (Juhe Feng)
Misty Screen Peak (Cuiping Feng)
Flying Phoenix Peak (Feifeng Feng)

Three more peaks may be glimpsed behind these:
Clean Altar Peak (Jingtan Feng)
Rising Cloud Peak (Qiyun Feng)
Mounting Aloft Peak (Shangsheng Feng)

More often than not these green-clad peaks are hidden by swirls of cloud and mist, and are difficult to distinguish, though each has its own characteristics and posture.

The most famous is the **Shennu Feng (Goddess Peak)**—also referred to as Observing the Clouds Peak—which resembles the figure of a maiden kneeling in front of a pillar. She is believed to be the embodiment of Yao Ji, the 23rd daughter of the Queen Mother of the West. Yao Ji, at the age of 18, was sent to oversee the Jade Pool of the Western Heaven, accompanied by 11 fairy handmaidens. But she found life there lonely and cold, and took to rambling among the mountains and rivers of the mortal world. Wushan became her favourite place, and there she established a small palace. Once, returning from a visit to the Eastern Sea on her floating cloud, she came upon 12 dragons playing havoc with the river and the mountains, and causing flooding and hardship in their wake. She summoned Da Yu the Great from his work on the Yellow River and, alighting from her cloud, presented him with a heavenly supernatural book. This endowed him with powers to call upon the wind, rain, thunder and lightning to move the earth, thus enabling his sacred ox to slash open the gorges (which is why all oxen have bent horns), and permit the waters to drain into the Eastern Sea. Yao Ji resolved to stay here with her 11 maidens to protect the boats from the dangerous rapids, the peasants' crops from damage, the woodcutters from wild animals, and to grow the fungus of longevity for the sick. Eventually these 12 maidens became the 12 sentinel peaks of Wu Gorge. There are, of course, many variations to this story.

As the river twists and turns, a mountain comes in to view, appearing as if it will block the way. This is **Congregated Immortals Peak**, on whose grey-white rock face can just be made out a carved inscription, known as the **Kongming Pai**, which legend attributed to the great third-century politician and strategist Zhuge

Liang (*see* page 42). However, it seems that the inscription was in fact carved during the Ming Dynasty by the local people to show their eternal respect and regard for this hero.

Five kilometres (three miles) below Kongming Pai on the south bank is the small trading town of **Peishi**, which marks the provincial border between Sichuan and Hubei. Guo Morou, a 20th-century poet, wrote that at this point 'the prow of one's boat is already in Hubei while the stern is still in Sichuan.'

Whitewashed villages cling to the mountain terraces which produce grain crops and fruits—apples, persimmons, peaches, apricots and Chinese chestnuts.

Just above the north-bank town of **Guandukou**—marking the end of Wu Gorge—was the site of the Flint Rapid (Huoyan Shi), which was very violent at high water, with limestone rocks jutting into the river like huge stone gates beckoning helpless craft. These, along with all the dangerous rocks in the shipping channel, were blown up in the 1950s. Besides rapids, other dangers to navigators included whirlpools, quicksand and currents which varied from hour to hour.

Badong

Badong, the county seat, has developed around one main street, extending from a power station at the eastern end to factories spreading along three or four hill slopes to the west. It is the westernmost county town of Hubei Province. Labourers, pitch black from coal-dust, with staff in hand, negotiate the steep slopes above the river, humping baskets of coal as they load and unload river lighters. Houses with wooden balconies huddle together on pillars embedded in solid concrete foundations above the bank of the river.

In ancient times, Badong was situated on the other side of the Yangzi and belonged to the State of Ba; in the Song dynasty (960–1279) the town was moved to the southern bank.

Badong has two pavilions of architectural interest—the **Autumn Wind Pavilion (Qiufeng Ting)** and the **White Cloud Pavilion (Baiyun Ting)**. Local products include tung oil, lacquer, tea, medicinal herbs and animal skins.

The **Shennong Xi (Stream)** is a small tributary of the Yangzi boasting gorges that rival those of the Daning River and is visited by many tourist ships as an alternative to the Daning. Depending on the season, an excursion may involve a two-hour bus ride to the head of the gorges. From here a team of trackers push and haul the wooden sampans over the shallow rapids until the Yangzi is reached some two hours later.

Zigui

Qu Yuan, one of China's greatly loved patriotic poets, was born in 340 BC in the Qu family village very near Zigui. The fame of the walled town on the north bank dates from this period long ago.

Qu Yuan's Memorial Hall, with its distinctive white gateway and walls edged in red, is visible on the hillside east of the town. It contains a Ming-dynasty (1368–1644) statue of the poet, as well as stone inscriptions.

The great poet served as a chancellor to King Huai of the Kingdom of Chu, with special responsibility for the royal clans. The king had complete trust in him until discord developed among the clans and Qu was falsely slandered. Banished from the capital, he wandered about in Hubei Province, deeply sad and bitter. His poetry and essays reveal his romanticism, loyalty and patriotism. Qu had vigorously advocated that the State of Chu stand firm against attack by the Qin state, but his advice had gone unheeded, and in May of the year 278 BC, he drowned himself in Dongting Lake at the age of 62.

According to historical records, the local people scoured Dongting Lake for his body, beating drums and racing their boats in the course of their search. This event came to be commemorated each May, and to this day the Dragon Boat Festival (Duanwu Jie) is held in the river towns up and down the Yangzi and in many other parts of China. *Zongzi*—packets of sweetened rice steamed in leaves and tied with reeds—were thrown into the water as a sacrifice to Qu Yuan. The tradition of eating *zongzi* at this festival continues, even in Beijing.

There are many fairy tales about Qu Yuan. East of Zigui is a bay named after him. It is said that when he died, a huge fish swallowed him up and swam all the way from Dongting Lake past Zigui to Yufu and back again, where it disgorged the body, amazingly still intact (*see also* page 55). In his home village is the Qu Field which he allegedly tilled. It is said that he never forgot his ancestral home; to the farmers there he introduced a jade-white rice which was soft and fragrant. Locals remember him at each new rice harvest.

■ XIANG XI (FRAGRANT STREAM)
A small stream just below Zigui and above the entrance to Xiling Gorge is well known to all Chinese as the home of the beautiful Han-dynasty (206 BC–AD 220) heroine Wang Zhaojun. Her story is the quintessence of virtuous patriotism.

Zhaojun, a maid of honour to the emperor, refused to bribe the painter from whose portraits of court ladies the emperor traditionally chose his concubines. In re-venge, the painter portrayed her as quite hideous, and so imperial favour was denied her. In 22 BC the emperor, wishing to make a marriage alliance with the northern Xiongnu king, chose Wang Zhaojun. Only then did he set eyes on her; he was captivated but it was too late. Married to the Xiongnu king, Zhaojun was

*Sampans on the Daning River tributary,
the only access to the hinterland of the Three Gorges region*

able to exert a good influence on relations between the Xiongnu and Han peoples, which gained her great respect. The emperor, in his rage at having lost her, decreed the beheading of the corrupt court painter. Local people say that before her marriage, Wang Zhaojun returned to her home town and, when washing in the stream, dropped a precious pearl which caused the stream to become crystal-clear and fragrant.

Xiling Gorge

Xiling Gorge starts at Xiang Xi and zigzags for 76 kilometres (47 miles) down to Yichang (see photograph on pages 80–81). It is the longest and historically the most dangerous of the Yangzi gorges. Before the passage was made safe in the 1950s, 'the whole surface of the water was a swirling mass of whirlpools sucking the froth they created into their centres.' Xiling comprises seven small gorges and two of the fiercest rapids in the stretch of the Yangzi between Chongqing and Yichang.

On entering the western entrance the boat passes through the 4-kilometre (2.4-mile) long **Military Books and Precious Sword Gorge (Bingshu Baojian Xia)**. The name of the gorge refers to a stratified layer of rock resembling a stack of books, and a perpendicular rock shaft below it, at a small cave on the north bank. There are two stories told of these formations, both concerning heroes from the classical novel *Romance of the Three Kingdoms* (*see* page 42).

One legend has it that Zhuge Liang (181–234), military adviser to the King of Shu, became seriously ill while passing this way. Unwilling to entrust his valuable military treatises to any member of his entourage, he placed them up here on this inaccessible ledge, to be kept safe for later generations. The second tale is also about Zhuge Liang. It was he who devised the stratagems which enabled Liu Bei, the king, to defeat the Kingdom of Chu and establish the Minor Han dynasty (AD 221–63). Afraid that he would eventually fall out of favour, Zhang Liang retired from official life and went into seclusion, hiding his military writings and sword here.

A large cleft rock stands at the mouth of a ravine—**Rice Granary Gorge (Micang Xia)**—on the south side. Fine sand, blown by river winds, piles up on this rock, and slowly sifts through a hole underneath. People call this Zhuge Liang's Granary.

Further on, the perilous **Xin Tan** or **New Rapid** rushes over submerged rocks, the oily surface of the water churned by whirlpools. In 1524, rock slides from the northern mountainside created this 3.2-kilometre (1.9-mile) long, triple-headed rapid. The fall of the riverbed had been estimated at about 6 metres (20 feet), but today it has a drop of only 2 metres (6.5 feet).

When the water level was low, junks would unload their cargo and be hauled over by 100 or more trackers. Passengers would join their boat beyond the rapid after walking along a winding mountain track and passing through the village of Xintan, once the site of the White Bone Pagoda—a giant pile of bleached bones, which was all that survived of the many thousands who had lost their lives at this frightening place. In 1941 the steamboat *Minxi* came to grief and several hundred people perished. The swift current carried boats downriver through Xin Tan at the rate of 7 metres (30 feet) per second.

In 1854 a local merchant collected subscriptions from river traders and built three life-saving craft to patrol this rapid, and to salvage boats and survivors. This was the beginning of the Yangzi River Lifeboat Office, which eventually maintained its red boats on all the danger spots along the Chongqing–Yichang stretch until the 1940s.

The channel winds east and then south, towards **Ox Liver and Horse Lungs Gorge**, apparently named after the yellow stalactite formations on the north side. One of the 'Horse's Lungs' is missing, blown up by British gunboats during the reign of Guangxu (1875–1908).

In the middle stretch of **Xiling Gorge**, the strangely lovely **Kongling Gorge** towers above the iron-green rocks of the 2.5-kilometre (1.5-mile) long **Kongling Tan**, the worst of all the Yangzi rapids. Seventeen catastrophes involving steamships occurred here between 1900 and 1945. The larger boulders choking the channel had names such as 'Big Pearl', 'Monk's Rock' and 'Chickens' Wings', but the deadliest of all was known as 'Come to Me'.

As the boat enters **Yellow Ox Gorge (Huangniu Xia)**—said to look like a man riding an ox—the passage widens out and sweeps under the ancient **Huangling Temple (Huangling Miao)** on the south face, nestling amid orange and pomelo trees. The great poet Du Fu wrote of his journey through this gorge:

Three dawns shine upon the Yellow Ox.
Three sunsets—and we go so slowly.
Three dawns—again three sunsets—
And we do not notice that our hair is white as silk.

Huangling Temple, said to have been first built during the Spring and Autumn period (770–476 BC), is dedicated to the great Dayu who, with his yellow ox, controlled the flood waters and dug the gorges (*see* page 39). The present hall was built in the Ming dynasty (1368–1644) and houses a statue of Da Yu, as well as stone inscriptions. Zhuge Liang is also said to have dug the Yellow Ox Spring (or Toad Rock, as it is sometimes called) nearby. Its clear water, according to the Tang-dynasty *Book of Teas*, was excellent for the brewing of tea, and Yellow Ox was classified as the Fourth Spring under Heaven.

After passing below Huangling Temple, the **Bright Moon Gorge (Mingyue Xia)** and the **Lantern Shadow Gorge (Dengying Xia)** loom ahead. The latter is overlooked on the south side by peaks in the shape of four figures from *Pilgrimage to the West* (also known as *Monkey*). When the evening sun's rays fall upon these peaks, the figures do appear lifelike—Xuan Zang standing on the precipice edge; Monkey (Sun Wukong) peering into the distance; Sandy (Sha Heshang) carrying the luggage; and Pigsy (Zhu Bajie) riding a horse, all silhouetted against the fading light like characters in a shadow play.

The last of the smaller gorges is **Yellow Cat Gorge (Huangmao Xia)**, so named from the yellow cat-shaped rock on the riverside. 'Qi Taigong Fishing' is the name given to a rock beside a cave on the south face, because of its fancied resemblance to a bearded old man wearing yellow trousers.

Now the boat reaches the strategic **Southern Crossing Pass (Nanjin Guan)**, with Three Travellers' Cave above (*see* page 89), marking the end of Xiling Gorge and the three great Yangzi gorges. The river widens dramatically and ahead lies Gezhouba Dam and Yichang.

River Rites
—by Madeleine Lynn

Life on board a junk was hard and dangerous work. Cornell Plant, River Inspector for the Chinese Imperial Maritime Service in the 1900s, wrote about the risks of travelling through the Three Gorges: Chinese say that one junk in ten is badly damaged, and one in 20 totally wrecked each trip. Probably not 20 percent reach Chungking unscathed, and never one without experiencing some hair-breadth escape.

It was common for trackers to fall from the tow-paths to their deaths or to break a limb and be left behind by their junk. Thus Yangzi boatmen had a wealth of rites and taboos that had to be observed to ensure a safe passage.

At the beginning of a voyage and also before entering the Three Gorges, the most dangerous stretch of the river, it was the cook's task to light incense, set off firecrackers and, most importantly, to kill a rooster and sprinkle the blood on the bows of the junk. Writing in 1880, Captain Gill described how to get through the Xintan Rapids safely. The junk could hire a shaman who would come on board with a yellow flag inscribed 'Power of the Water! A happy star for the whole journey'. As the boat ploughed through the waves dragged by the straining trackers, the shaman would stand at the bow, waving the flag in a regular motion to appease the powers of the water. It was also essential to sprinkle rice on the water all the way through the rapids.

Like fishermen everywhere in China, many Yangzi boatmen still believe that it is very bad luck to turn over a fish at table: 'capsize fish, capsize boat'. Another taboo is resting chopsticks on top of a rice bowl in a position that suggests a junk ran aground. Unlike Western sailors, however, there is no taboo against women aboard ship and junk owners usually brought their wives along.

Sometimes fish swimming upstream used to jump onto the decks. They were considered demons and had to be taken ashore and buried. Boatmen also had to contend with the ghosts of the drowned, who would string them-

83

selves in a line behind a boat, preparing to board the vessel and cause trouble. The way to shake them lose was to cut quickly in front of another boat,
so that the ghosts would lose their grip and attach themselves to the boat
behind. Not a very neighbourly thing to do! Describing this to explorer
Wong How Man in 1986, a boat captain recounted that 'In the past, it was a
game that often left the trailing boat's owner jumping, cursing and shooting
off firecrackers to pacify his increased string of ghosts'.

Meanwhile those living on shore had floods to contend with. The lovely
pagodas all along the river were built for flood prevention. It was believed
that floods were often caused by dragons (since they have the power to
control the waters), or by evil demons. A pagoda built on top of the hill
inhabited by one of these creatures could prevent him from coming out and
causing trouble. A pagoda could also prevent the wealth of the nearby town
from being swept away by the current.

After the disastrous flood of 1788, which inundated over 30 counties in
Hubei Province, the Emperor ordered nine iron oxen to be placed along the
banks of the river. According to the court record: 'The Sea Dragon submits
to Iron and the Ox belongs to Earth, Earth controls Water, the Iron Ox can
suppress the flood'. This was following Chinese theories of the properties of
the elements: fire, metal, earth and water.

■ GEZHOUBA DAM

The massive 20-metre (66-foot) high Gezhouba Dam arrests the Yangzi's flow
and forces all shipping up and down the gorges to pass through one of its three
ship locks. With 21 power generators and a total capacity of 2.715 million kilo-
watts per hour, the dam is the largest in China so far. It will be surpassed by the
planned Three Gorges Dam, however, about 40 kilometres upstream (*see* page
62). The dam consists of locks, silt-prevention dikes, silt-clearing sluices, spill-
ways and power plants. Visitors to Yichang (*see* pages 86–87) can visit a centre
near the dam site which has a model of the dam and a video on the subject—
plus the inevitable souvenir shop.

The Middle Reaches: Yichang to Hukou

From Yichang the Yangzi enters its middle basin, flowing for 1,010 kilometres (630 miles) to the mouth of Poyang Lake in Jiangxi Province. The river, widening out abruptly from the narrow confines of Xiling Gorge and with a pent-up force out of Gezhouba Dam, rolls through broad floodplains, fed by tributaries and lakes that become serious flood points during heavy summer rains.

Networks of dikes and embankments—obscuring the view—stretch the length of the river, which can be as wide as 1.5 to 2 kilometres (1 to 1.3 miles), and can even today cause widespread flooding during normal rainy seasons. In abnormal summer deluges the many lakes in the area, joining forces with the Yangzi and its tributaries, inundate the land, forming great expanses of water. This must have been the situation observed by two great foreign travellers in China: Marco Polo in the 13th century and the French Lazarist priest, Abbé Huc, in the 18th century, both of whom recorded the Yangzi as being more than 15 kilometres (9 miles) wide.

Up to the Sui dynasty (581–618) the middle reaches were sparsely inhabited, but from the Tang dynasty (618–907) on, waves of people migrated from the north, fleeing from civil wars, famines, heavy taxation and harassment from marauding Tibetans and Turks. With the sharp rise in population, dike construction became more intense. But it was during the Ming and Qing dynasties (1368–1644 and 1644–1911) that treasury funds were allocated to the construction of dikes—mainly along the north bank of the Yangzi—which were built as high as 10–16 metres (33–52 feet) in places. Once built, the burden of maintenance fell to local landowners and peasants, and upkeep was often neglected.

The meandering, looping course of the river creates severe silting so that the raised riverbed requires constant dredging, and as large boats crisscross the channel, their wash churns into the embankment causing mini-landslides. The rich alluvial Jianghan Plain, between the north bank of the Yangzi and the Han River, is a major cotton- and grain-growing area very vulnerable to flooding. In 1952 the Jingjiang Flood Diversion Project was launched. Flood prevention measures included the strengthening of the 180-kilometre (110 mile) stretch of dike along the Yangzi's northern bank (in the Shashi region), and the construction of flood-intake sluices, regulating dams and retention basins on the south side to divert the waters. On the Han River, the Danjiangkou Water Conservancy Project and dam draw the flood waters from this tributary to irrigate the more arid regions of northwest Hubei. The Shashi retention basin, covering an area of 920 square kilometres (355 square miles), took 300,000 workers some 75 days to construct in 1954.

(previous pages) Bellows Cave in Qutang Gorge near Baidi Cheng, with a narrow trackers path cut into the cliff-side on the right

Above Dongting Lake, the Yangzi forms the border between the provinces of Hubei and Hunan. The lake is the second largest in China. Fed by four rivers and emptying its waters into the Yangzi, it abounds in aquatic products. At Dongting Lake the river streaks northeastwards, beside hinterland dotted with numerous lakes, towards Wuhan, the largest city along its middle reaches. Here it is joined by the 1,532-kilometre (952-mile) long Han River.

During the dry winters, shifting sandbars and low water levels pose serious hazards to shipping. At Wuhan, the navigation channel can be as shallow as 2 metres (6.5 feet). Estimates put the volume of silt passing Wuhan each year at more than 140 million cubic metres (183 million cubic yards).

Freshwater fish abound—silver and big-head carp, Yangzi sturgeon, Wuchang fish and giant salamander, to name a few. Native to the river are dolphins and a species of alligator, though both of these are extremely rare today.

Having crossed the entire width of Hubei Province, the river enters Jiangxi, forming its border with Anhui. Immediately below the city of Jiujiang and the cherished, beautiful mountain of Lushan, it is joined by the blue freshwaters of Poyang Lake, the biggest in all of China. From here on, the Yangzi enters its lower reaches.

The river traffic is light, mostly convoys of barges or boats linked to a single tugboat, dredgers excavating the navigational channels, and fishing *sampans* with patched sails.

Steamer ferries stop briefly at the coal-mining town of **Zhicheng** and pass under one of the few bridges that span the Yangzi.

Yichang

Situated at the eastern mouth of the gorges, Yichang is the administrative centre of nine surrounding counties. Its population is engaged in light industry, chemical and steel production. The construction of the **Gezhouba Dam** helped Yichang to grow from a small town of 30,000 into a city, and about 10 percent of the investment capital for the proposed Three Gorges Dam, only 44 kilometres (27 miles) upstream, will be poured into the Yichang administrative region. Thus although some houses and factories will be submerged, a plethora of new buildings are being built higher up, in anticipation of the boom. There are plans for a new airport, a bridge across the Yangzi, new roads and railway lines.

HISTORY OF YICHANG
History records that as early as 278 BC the town was razed to the ground in a battle between the armies of Chu and Qin. In the Three Kingdoms period (*see*

page 42) 50,000 Wu troops set fire to the encampments of the Shu army, utterly routing Liu Bei, who retreated upriver to Baidi Cheng (*see* page 56).

Yichang was the trans-shipment point for cargo up and down the river. Here, cargo was unloaded from the larger boats plying the stretch of river between Yichang and Wuhan, and reloaded onto smaller ones running between Yichang and Chongqing. An American traveller in 1921 described the port as 'crowded, incessantly busy, a perfect maelstrom of sampans, junks, lighters with cargo, steamers and gunboats.' It was declared a foreign Treaty Port in 1876.

The English trader Archibald Little, noting his expenses for a night's stay in the Treaty Port, showed how far four English pennies went in late 19th-century Yichang, and incidentally his solicitude for his servant:

Supper for self and coolie, 4 bowls of rice at 10 cash (copper cash), 'fixings' of cabbage and bean curd free	40
Use of straw-plaited mattress for ditto, 2 at 10	20
Breakfast, same as supper	40
Supper and breakfast for 'Nigger', my dog	20
Pair of straw sandals for coolie (his old ones being worn out)	12
Total 132 copper cash, or, in English money, 4d	132

During the warlord years of the early part of this century, Yichang's revenue was greatly boosted by taxes imposed on boats carrying homegrown opium from Yunnan and Guizhou Provinces by its Opium Suppression Bureau.

When Wuhan fell to the Japanese in 1938, Yichang became the centre for shipping essential personnel, machinery, libraries and museum collections up the Yangzi to Chongqing. After the Battle of Yichang in 1940, the Japanese used Yichang as a staging area for bombing raids over Chongqing.

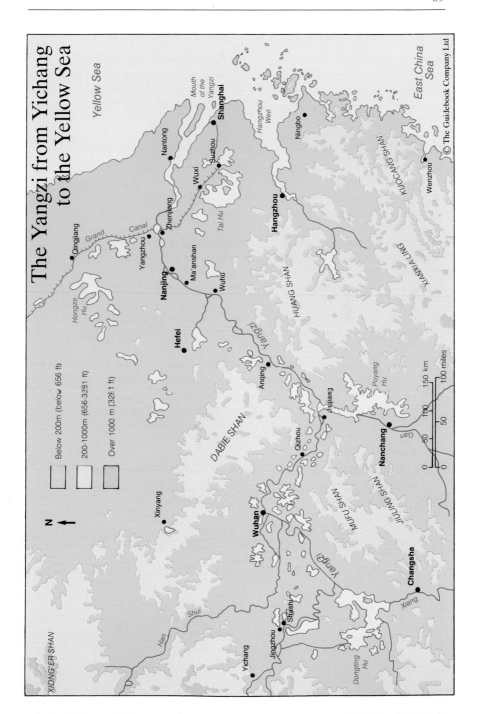

The Yangzi from Yichang to the Yellow Sea

Yellow Sea

East China Sea

© The Guidebook Company Ltd

Mouth of the Yangzi

Shanghai

Nantong

Suzhou

Wuxi

Zhenjiang

Hangzhou Wen

Ningbo

Wenzhou

KUOCANG SHAN

Qingjiang

Grand Canal

Yangzhou

Nanjing

Ma'anshan

Wuhu

Tai Hu

HUANG SHAN

XIANXI LING

Hongze Hu

Hefei

Yangzi

Anqing

Poyang Hu

Jiujiang

Nanchang

Gan

Qizhou

DABIE SHAN

JIULING SHAN

MUFU SHAN

Xinyang

N

Below 200m (below 656 ft)

200-1000m (656-3281 ft)

Over 1000 m (3281 ft)

150 km

100 miles

Wuhan

Yangzi

Changsha

Xiang

Shashi

Jingzhou

Yichang

Han

Shui

Dongting Hu

XIONG'ER SHAN

WHAT TO SEE IN YICHANG

The streets of the old town centre are lined with trees. Though the city wall was pulled down in 1929, the street names still indicate where it once stood (Eastern Ring Road, Southern Ring Road and so on). The main market is found just off Jiefang Lu. Along the waterfront a few old foreign buildings of the Treaty Port days can be seen.

Apart from the Gezhouba Dam (*see* page 83), tourists may also visit the **Three Travellers Cave**, 10 kilometres (6 miles) northwest of the city. In 819, three Tang-dynasty poets, Bai Zhuyi, his brother Bai Xingjian and Yuan Zhen, met up in Yichang and made an excursion to this site. While enjoying the spectacular scenery, they inscribed some poems on the cave walls. Afterwards they were dubbed the 'First Three Travellers'. In the Song dynasty (960–1279) the famous literary family of Su—the father and two sons—on their way to the capital to take the imperial examinations, visited the cave and added poems as well. All three passed the imperial examinations at the same time. People call these gentlemen the 'Second Three Travellers'. Throughout the ages, other visiting literati and officials have left their contributions on the cave walls.

A small spring trickles through the rock near the entrance; local superstition maintains that if women wash their hands in its pure water it will improve their culinary skills. The hill above the cave presents a fine view of the entrance to Xiling Gorge: The Zixi Pavilion contains a memorial stone to the llth-century philosopher Ouyang Xiu, who lived in Yichang for three years. Nearby is a drum platform said to be the site where Zhang Fei (*see* page 42), a general of the third century AD State of Shu, beat his battle drums.

Visitors are usually taken on a short excursion along a mountain road offering stunning views of Xiling Gorge, and passing several peaks, including Filial Mountain and Camel Mountain. The road continues over a natural stone bridge, which was originally—so legend has it—a fairy's silken sash, thrown up to help her mortal husband ascend to heaven with her. The stone gateway and its steep stone steps delineate the ancient land route crossed by travellers to western Hubei and Sichuan.

Below Yichang lies the bluff known as Tiger's Teeth Gorge which, for travellers upriver, is the first glimpse of sights to come.

Jingzhou

Jingzhou, previously the famous city of Jiangling, has now been somewhat absorbed by the sprawling growth of Shashi, but it is still surrounded by its 16-kilometre (10-mile) long and 9-metre (30-foot) high city wall. Jingzhou is visited from Shashi.

Jingzhou was the capital of Jing, one of the nine great regions into which Emperor Yu, founder of the Xia dynasty (2205–1766 BC), divided China. From Jingzhou the emperor received as tribute exotic gifts of gold, ivory, cinnabar, silver and feathers.

In the Spring and Autumn period (770–476 BC) the city was the capital of the Kingdom of Chu. Its walls, according to tradition, were first built in the third century by Guan Yu, a hero of the Three Kingdoms era. Guan Yu was renowned for his strength, height and valour. A thousand years after his death he was deified as the god of war, and his fierce red-faced image appears in many Chinese temples throughout Asia. Stories of his exploits and battles over the city are vividly told in the novel, *Romance of the Three Kingdoms* (*see* page 42).

WHAT TO SEE IN JINGZHOU
Since Jingzhou was the capital of 20 kingdoms during both the Spring and Autumn and Warring States periods, it is not surprising that valuable artefacts have been found buried in the many tombs on Phoenix Hill. These relics, in particular an important collection of lacquerware, 2,000-year-old silk garments and fabrics, and an almost perfectly preserved male corpse of a Han-dynasty official, are exhibited at the **Jingzhou Museum**. The museum is one of the best in all China as well as an important research centre, and is well worth a visit.

Shashi

Shashi is situated on the north bank of the Yangzi, and its cotton mills are supplied with raw cotton from the rich Jianghan Plain on which it stands. Shashi's population of 240,000 is principally employed in its many light-industrial enterprises—machinery, durable consumer goods, printing, dyeing and textiles. Tourist boats frequently stop in Shashi for a visit to the ancient walled city of Jingzhou nearby.

The city was the port for the ancient city of Jiangling and a distribution centre for produce from surrounding towns and Dongting Lake, which was trans-shipped mostly to Wuhan. This trade was in cotton, beans, grain and aquatic products. In the Tang dynasty (618–907) it already enjoyed a reputation as a prosperous city, but its peak was reached during the years of the Taiping Rebellion, in the mid-19th century (*see* page 116). After the rebels captured Nanjing in 1853, river trade on the Yangzi between Shashi and Shanghai more or less came to a standstill, so Shashi became vital to the distribution of products coming downriver from Sichuan.

The Sino-Japanese Treaty of 1895 opened the city to foreign trade; Japanese engaged in the cotton-seed trade formed the majority of the resident foreigners, though this community was never large.

There is a story that the army of Communist General Ho Lung captured Swedish missionaries here in 1931. The women were released following negotiations with the Swedish Consul-General, but the release of a doctor was delayed until a ransom was paid. The ransom demanded was: four dozen Parker fountainpens, four dozen watches and 60 or 70 cases of medical drugs!

West of the city, the seven-storeyed **Wanshoubao Pagoda**, built in the Ming dynasty (1368–1644), stands directly on the waterfront. Bas-relief figures of Buddha, set into niches, and inscriptions by the donors adorn its brick facade. A monastery once adjoined it.

Below Shashi the river winds tortuously towards Dongting Lake for about 320 kilometres (200 miles). Villages dot the south bank of the river and water buffalo graze in the paddy fields. The north embankment is often too high for a view of the surrounding country.

DONGTING LAKE

The beautiful Dongting Lake is rich in fairy tales and legends. On its eastern shore stands the graceful three-storey **Yueyang Tower** of Yueyang City, one of the Three Great Towers south of the Yangzi (the other two being Yellow Crane Tower in Wuchang, and Prince Teng Pavilion in Nanchang). From its terraces and from pleasure boats on the lake, many famous Chinese poets have been moved to verse.

> The lake embraces distant hills and devours the Yangzi, its mighty waves rolling endlessly.
> From morning glow to evening light, the views change a thousand, ten thousand times.
> On top of the tower the mind relaxes, the heart delights.
> All honours and disgrace are forgotten.
> What pleasure, what joy to sit here and drink in the breeze.
>
> Fan Zhongyan (989–1052)

Said to have been constructed on the site of a reviewing platform for navy manoeuvres on the lake during the third century, the first tower was erected in 716. The present golden-tiled, square tower dates from 1985, but it has been rebuilt in the Song-dynasty style at great expense.

Legend has it that the tower was saved from collapse by the supernatural powers of Lu Dongbin, a Daoist (Taoist) Immortal, who also got drunk here three times. These occasions are remembered in the form of the Thrice Drunken Pavilion, which flanks the tower.

An excursion on to the lake can be made to **Junshan Island**, 15 kilometres (9 miles) away. Some 4,000 years ago, Emperor Shun, on an inspection tour, died at

Mount Jiuyi on the south bank of the lake. Two of his devoted concubines, hurrying to his side, became stranded on Junshan Island. The story goes that in their distress, their copious tears blotted the local bamboo, henceforth known as the Spotted Bamboo of Junshan. They drowned themselves in the lake, and their graves remain. In 219 BC, Emperor Qin Shihuangdi, also on a tour of Dongting Lake, was delayed at Junshan Island by a sudden storm. When he consulted his geomancer as to whether spirits were impeding his progress, he was told of the concubines' graves. In a fury he ordered the burning of the island and had five stone seals placed there, forbidding its name to be used or anyone to visit it.

On the 100-hectare (250-acre) island, Junshan Silver Needle Tea is grown, so highly prized that it was once presented as a tribute to the imperial court.

Once China's largest freshwater lake, the Dongting now ranks second, due to sandbars and silt accumulation from the four rivers which feed it. As a result of flood prevention schemes—6,100 irrigation and drainage channels and 15,000 sluices—the surrounding land has become productive all year round and the lake acts as a reservoir for summer flood waters. The 3,000-square kilometre (1,160-square mile) lake abounds in fish.

Luxury goods from Canton—from pearls to kingfisher feathers—reached the ancient capitals by way of the Xiang River, through Dongting Lake, down the Yangzi to Yangzhou and then on up the Grand Canal.

Three Kingdoms' Red Cliff

From the flat bank appears a sharp rock escarpment dotted with pavilions and paths. This is the site of the great Battle of the Red Cliff between the huge forces of Cao Cao of Wei and the combined, lesser armies of Shu and Wu in AD 208. Cao Cao had consolidated the power of the Kingdom of Wei in the north and sought to extend it to the Yangzi. His troops, all from the northern plains, were not accustomed to naval warfare. Nevertheless, he took his army of 200,000 men to launch his attack on the Kingdom of Shu, whose king, Liu Bei, called upon the King of Wu for assistance.

In urgent need of 100,000 arrows to repel the invaders, Zhuge Liang (adviser to Liu Bei) devised a brilliant stratagem. Twenty naval junks, beating war drums, but stacked high with only bundles of straw shrouded in black cloth, feigned an advance on the Wei encampment on a dark, foggy night. The Wei commanders responded by discharging their arrows into the indistinct hulks on the junks. By dawn, each junk bristled with thousands of arrows, more than enough for the army's requirements.

By another ruse, Cao Cao was persuaded by a spy in his camp to secure all his boats together for a forthcoming attack, so that his soldiers would feel as if they were on firm ground. The armies of Wu and Shu set fire to the boats in the midst of the battle and, with a favourable wind, the great conflagration brought about the defeat of Cao Cao, who fled northwards.

Red Cliff itself is said to have been forever scorched red by the flames of this day-long battle. In a victory celebration, General Zhou Yu of Wu, flourishing his writing brush, jubilantly inscribed the gigantic characters 'Red Cliff' (Chi Bi) on the cliff face, which can be seen to this day.

Pavilions on the hill commemorate specific incidents in the battle, and there is an exhibition of over 2,000 weapons, dating from the Three Kingdoms period, that were found in the area. The story of the battle is known to all Chinese, and this makes the site a very popular tourist spot.

HAN RIVER

The Han River, at 1,532 kilometres, or 952 miles, the Yangzi's longest tributary, rises in the Qingling Mountains of Shaanxi Province. In 1488 it changed its course, separating the city of Hanyang from the fishing village of Hankou, as it then was. Though dikes line much of its lower course, this stretch has a history of frequent flooding. The British consular officer, August R. Margary, who travelled all the way from Shanghai up the Yangzi and on to the Burmese border in 1876, only to be murdered by tribesmen as he crossed back into China, wrote of Hankou:

> This year they have had no inundation, but it is of almost annual occurrence. Even at Hankow the foreign settlement is frequently submerged. The river rises six feet above the level of the fine stone bund they have made there, and quietly takes possession of all the lower rooms in the noble-looking mansions which the merchants occupy. All their dining-room furniture has to be removed above. Boats become the only means of locomotion, and ladies can be seen canoeing in and out of their houses, and over the bund where they are wont to promenade at other times.

Flooding occurred 11 times from 1931 to 1949; in 1931 and 1935 boats sailed down the streets of Wuhan. Though much has been done in recent years to control the Han's waters, the danger of flooding is still very real.

Wuhan

At the centre of the Long River's course to the sea and on the main rail line between north and south China sprawls the tripartite city of Wuhan. On the north bank lies Hankou, the commercial centre and port complex, now gleaming with a new skyline sprouting along its broad avenues. Across the Han River flowing from the north is Hanyang, known for the Turtle Hill overlooking the No.1 Yangzi River Bridge and the Qing Chuan Temple. Upriver in Hanyang are vast steel plants and factories. On the south bank of the Yangzi are the administrative and educational campuses of Wuchang, the seat of the Hubei Provincial Government and Wuhan University. The Yellow Crane Tower, the symbol of the Wuhan, rises above the Great River at Wuchang at the foot of the bridge.

Wuhan is set in the vast Jiang Han Plain, a region that is more water than land. Levees protect the city from the seasonal ravages of the Yangzi. One may dock in summer flood season to walk down gangways onto the dikes and then down to street level. A giant new passenger ship terminal in Hankou is shaped like a cartoon image of a ship, from whence stream thousands of travellers from the sharp prowed transport ships from Shanghai and Chongqing. Deluxe cruise ships—Chinese style—tie up with their flashing karaoke club lights and "welcome" maidens wearing silk *chipaos* on the gangway.

The former British Customs House clock tower remains at waters edge, now topped with a red star. Its prominence is now eclipsed by mirrored nightclubs such as the 'Formosa' and recently a new 'Sailor's Club' faced with a three story bronze lion's visage. New hotels line the waterfront where clipper ships once loaded tea. The jumbled old neighborhoods and alleyways where foreign sailors once entered at their own risk are being torn down for ever grander shopping malls. The alley from the old Customs House up to Zhong Shan Da Dao—Sun Yatsen Way—is being upgraded to the likes of McDonald's. Many of the graceful European style buildings of the early century are being replaced with bloated glass walled towers.

One can still hop on bicycle pedicabs to wind through the neighborhood street markets, which are being chased out by development. In the remaining old sections, the most interesting parts are too narrow for bikes, but good to walk. Watch your step! The local cuisine is rich in aquatic products including snails, frogs, eels and myriad pond and river fish. Rats are also trapped for their nutritional value.

Vast new business complexes have been built in the northern reaches of Hankou. A new international airport is open just north of the city limits with a direct expressway. The new No.2 Yangzi River Bridge was opened in 1996, its high wired spires linking Hankou with Wuchang downriver, easing the bottleneck of the old bridge and impelling urbanization of the eastern suburbs. As the city economy continues to grow, much of the old city is being lost to redevelopment, and as in much of China, the new construction lacks the social web of the old neighborhoods, though many of the traditional fragrances remain.

The calm reaches of Wuchang's East Lake with its bonsai gardens and excellent museums are the best antidote to the smoggy hubbub of the downtown districts.

HISTORY OF WUHAN
The area on which Wuhan stands was settled in the first century; in the third century it was part of the Kingdom of Wu. Wuchang is the oldest of the three cities. By the Yuan dynasty (1279–1368) it was the capital of the region and was enclosed by a city wall until the end of the 19th century.

Hanyang was founded in the Sui dynasty (581–618) and remained a small walled

Wuhan

to Beijing

Hankou
Railway Station

Huangpu

Jiefang Park

Jiefang Gongyuan Lu

Ouchang Lu

Xinhua

Dadao

Former
the Eig
Army C

Hanyang Lu

Yanjiang

International Trade
Centre Mansion

Chezhan Lu

CITS Wuhan Branch
Binjiang F

HANKOU

Zhongshan
Park

Jianghan Beilu

Zhongshan

Shengli

Dadao

Railway
Ticket Office

Shanghai Bund
Hotel

Shanghai Bund

Hangkong Lu

Wuhan
Medical College

Changjiang
Hotel

Wuhan
Exhibition Hall

Xuangong
Hotel

Foreign Languages Bookstore

Zhongshan Lu

Wuhan
Market

Antiques and
Cunos Store

Jianghan Lu

CITS Changjiang Branc

Jiefang

CAAC
Booking Office

Minsheng Lu

Wuhan Customhouse

Wuhan
Gymnasium

Asia Hotel

Wuhan Arts
and Crafts Shop

Minquan Lu

Passenger Terminal

Qiaokou

Wusheng

Liji Lu

Dadao

Minzu Lu

Yanjiang

Han

Zhongshan

Lu

Lu

River

Jianghan Bridge

Dadao

Yuehu Lake
(Moon Lake)

Tortoise Hill

Qingchuan
Hotel

Linjiang

Peasant Move
Mao Zedong's
Former Reside

Hanyang

Lute Platform

Macang Lake

Hanyang
Railway Station

Dadao

Lianhua
(Lotus)
Lake

Wuhan Changjiang Bridge

Wuchang
Hotel

SIMENKOU

ZHONGJIA CUN

Lanjiang Lu

Huanghelou

Minzu Lu

Guixuan
Monastery

Snake Hill

Wuhan Zoo

Dadao

Yangzi

Lu

Railway
Ticket Office

Moshui Lake

HANYANG

Wuchang
Stadium

Ziyang Lu

Yingwu

Jiefang

Ziyang
Lake

Jiefang
Bridge

Qiyi (Uprising)
Gate

Xunshi

0   500   1000 1500 m
0   500   1000 1500 yards

★ Hotel

River

to C

ang'an Station

Dadao

Dadao

Linjiang

Simei Pond

XUJIAPENG

Heping

N

Donghu Lake (East Lake)

Lu

Changtian Tower

Lakeside Gallery

Huguang
(Lake Scenery)
Pavilion

DONGHU SCENIC AREA

Shahu Lake

Hubei Provincial
Museum

Xingyin (Strolling
and Reciting Pavilion

Front Gate of
Donghu Lake

Tingtao (Billow-Listening) House

Shuiyunxiang (Water-Cloud Country) House

ute Museum

Zhongbei

Donghu Lake (East Lake)

Lu

WUCHANG

Hongshan
Gymnasium

Shuiguo Lake

Hongshan
Auditorium

Hongshan Lu

Dongxu

Lu

Moshan Hill Botanical Gardens

Donghu

Minzu Lu

Zhongnan Lu

Zhongnan
Commercial
Building

Wuluo

Bayi

Hongshan Hill

Hongshan
Pagoda

Luojia Hill

Lu

Wuchang
Railway Station

Shaihu Lake

Lu

Luoshi

Lu

★ Swan Hotel

GUANGBUTUN

Luoyu

Lu

Laiwang Hill

Yujia Hill

city until a farsighted official of the Qing dynasty (1644–1911), Zhang Zhidong, established factories and an arsenal there in the 1890s. Hankou was only a fishing village until the 19th century.

It is, however, the city of Hankou which is best known to foreigners, for after it was declared a Treaty Port in 1861 it became a major centre of the tea trade and the focal point of the annual China Tea Races (*see* page 100).

There were five Foreign Concessions—British, Russian, French, German and Japanese—situated side by side along the north embankment of the Yangzi. Ocean-going steamers from New York, Odessa and London anchored at their docks. Until the foreign import of opium ceased in the first decade of this century, opium-laden ships sailed up the river as far as Hankou.

Life in the foreign concessions was similar to that in Shanghai. Horse-racing was popular, with Hankou boasting two racecourses, one for Chinese and one for foreigners. There was even a golf course, while the Recreation Club was considered by many to be the best in China at that time.

In the 1911 Revolution, much of Hankou was burnt to the ground during clashes between revolutionaries and imperial troops.

After the fall of the capital, Nanjing, in 1937 to the Japanese during the Sino-Japanese War, the Guomindang government made Wuhan its capital for a year, before moving to Chongqing. In the 1938 assault on Wuhan, casualty figures were in the tens of thousands.

The Communist Party was very active in Wuhan before 1949, organizing railway strikes and peasant training programmes. It was here that Chairman Mao, at the age of 73, took his famous 15-kilometre (9-mile) swim in the Yangzi during the Cultural Revolution days of 1966 (*see* page 106).

WHAT TO SEE IN WUHAN

■ HANKOU

Hankou is the main commercial area of Wuhan. Between its long main shopping street, Zhongshan Dadao, and the high embankment along the river are numerous street markets. The old foreign concessions line the embankment for 3 kilometres (2 miles) and this area is still very much intact. The vicinity of Hankou Railway Station is always busy and interesting to walk around. The old Customs House on the waterfront is a distinctive landmark. Jiefang Park and Zhongshan Park, across the railway line, are the sites of the former racecourses.

■ HANYANG
LUTE PLATFORM (GUQIN TAI)
Opposite Tortoise Hill, which overlooks the Han River, is the Hanyang Workers

Cultural Palace Gardens, encompassing the charming Lute Platform, a small complex of courtyards, pavilions and gardens enclosed by a tiled wall. It was built in commemoration of two musicians, Yu Baiya and Zhong Ziqi, who lived 2,000 years ago. While visiting Hanyang, Yu played his lute but only Zhong understood and appreciated his performance. They became fast friends and arranged to meet again at the same time the following year. Yu returned only to find that his friend had died. At Zhong's grave, Yu played a farewell song and, vowing never again to use the instrument, broke its strings.

The Lute Platform is now a haven for Chinese-opera lovers (mostly men) who gather on Sunday mornings to sip tea and listen to the performers. In the gardens, *wushu* (martial arts) and *taijiquan* (exercise classes) are held. Paintings by local artists are on exhibition and for sale in the main hall. Nearby is a Qing memorial stone dedicated to the lute player.

GUIYUAN MONASTERY
This fine Zen Buddhist monastery on Cuiwei Lu, where monks from the surrounding provinces gathered to study the scriptures, is 300 years old. The striking architectural complex includes Drum and Bell Towers, temple halls, the Luohan Hall and the Lotus Pond. The Luohan Hall contains 500 gold-painted wooden statues of Buddhist monk-saints; no two are the same. It is said the two sculptors employed on this task took nine years to complete it. The monastery runs a vegetarian restaurant, the Yunjizhai, for visitors.

■ WUCHANG
YELLOW CRANE TOWER
On Snake Hill is the site of the ancient Yellow Crane Tower, widely celebrated by Chinese poets throughout the ages. The legend concerns a Daoist (Taoist) sage who flew away on a yellow crane to become an Immortal. The tower has been rebuilt many times. Beside the new Yellow Crane Tower (completed in 1986) is a White *stupa* that dates from the Yuan dynasty (1279–1368).

HUBEI PROVINCIAL MUSEUM
Off Donghu Lu, near East Lake, this small museum has a rich collection of artifacts excavated in the province. Of special interest is a display of finds from the tomb of the Marquis Yi of Zeng from the Warring States period (475–221 BC). Among them is a set of 65 bronze chime bells. Replicas of these have been made and concerts of ancient music are given by a special chime-bells orchestra under the auspices of the Hubei Provincial Museum and Art Institute of Wuhan. The second floor of the museum is devoted to the province's revolutionary history.

THE HANKOW TEA RACES —Judy Bonavia

The handsome, full-sailed tea clippers which plied the high seas between China and Britain from the 18th to the 19th century were initially confined to the coastal ports—first Canton, then Shanghai and eventually Fuzhou. As the British East India Company lost its monopoly and the tea trade gathered momentum, so did the competition between shipping companies, particularly as the quality of the tea could deteriorate on a long sea journey. The fastest ships charged the highest freight rates in this lucrative trade. This was the origin of the annual China Tea Races, first in elegant clippers and later in the early steamships.

Following the opening of the Yangzi River cities to foreign trade after the 1858 Treaty of Tientsin (Tianjin), the first tea clipper, the *Challenger*, reached Hankou in 1861.

The introduction of the steamship in the middle of the 19th century saw an end to these romantic sailing ships, and the opening of the Suez Canal in 1869 greatly reduced the sailing time. Nevertheless, the Hankow (Hankou) Tea Races continued. Each May, tea buyers, known as *chazi*, came to Hankou as the ships began to arrive from England, Russia and America. The Hankow (Hankou) Club, sprang to life, with the Russian *chazi* drinking only champagne throughout the season. As many as 16 or 17 vessels would make up the British fleet, of which only two or three would be hot favourites and allowed to charge the highest freight rates.

Loaded with their cargo of black and green tea, the race began. The first leg from Hankou to the Red Buoy at Wusong (near Shanghai) could take as little as 36 hours if the ships did not run aground; then down the South China Sea to Singapore, where time was always lost in stockpiling coal for the last leg to London. In the 1877 race, two ships passed the Red Buoy together and reached Singapore with only 1 hour and 40 minutes between them. One ship lost six hours in port and arrived in London only 23 hours behind the winner after an exciting voyage of 31 days.

As the first ships were sighted in the English Channel, word was sent to the London brokers who would rush to the docks as the vessels berthed. In great excitement the tea chests were broken open for samples which were hurried off for inspection by the various buyers.

By the late 1880s India had moved into the lead of tea-exporting countries. The collapse of the China tea market brought about the end of a romantic era.

Picking tea leaves, gouache on pith paper, c. 1870

Tea manufacture, gouache on pith paper, c. 1870

A Hankow Flood

On the outskirts of Hankow, nearly all the so-called Chinese houses—
or, more correctly speaking, all the most miserable shanties, letting in
both wind and rain—on the bank of the river, are raised well up on
piles, thirty to forty feet above high-water mark; narrow wooden
pathways, running between the rows of houses, and small bridges
connecting these pathways where the houses are not continuous. In
these wretched dwellings live some hundreds of families, to all appearance without a care, and in the greatest state of contentment. Their
business, whatever it may be, is mostly connected with boats and junks,
for each house possesses either a sampan or a small, home-made, flat-
bottomed boat, mostly rotten and leaky, which is continually bringing
its occupants to grief, and when not in use is moored to the lower end
of the piles. The owners ascend and descend by means of some iron
spikes, driven in alternatively on either side of one of the piles.

There is in times of flood the greatest distress among the riverside
population. When the water rises twenty-five, thirty, or more feet above
its ordinary level, many of these piles are swept away, down come the
houses, bringing their occupants with them, who are carried away in
the current. Whatever becomes of the remains of these unfortunates, no
one seems to know or to care; not one in twenty is recovered, or ever seen
again. Of course there is great lamentation among the survivors for the
next week; crackers are let off by the thousand, small floating fires are
set adrift on the stream to pacify the river god, gongs are beaten, and
altogether the priests have a busy time.

So little value do the Chinese set upon human life in disasters of this
description, which are of yearly occurrence in one part of the Empire
or another, that the whole thing is soon forgotten, a fresh crowd
occupies the places of the former crowd, piles are re-driven, shanties rebuilt, and so the new lot live their careless, contented lives till, history
repeating itself, these people follow the lead of their predecessors.

In the early summer of 1887, the Bothwell Castle, a large ocean-
going steamer of three thousand tons, was lying at anchor opposite

Hankow, waiting for a cargo of tea. She had already been there two or
three weeks, and was likely to remain two or three more; the weather
being very bad, she made her holding secure with two anchors and a
great length of cable. Before receiving her full cargo, one of these sudden
floods occurred, and a week or two later I received from Captain Tod
the following account of the disaster. He said:

One morning, shortly after breakfast, we heard a rumbling noise far
away up the stream, and not long after an immense rush of water, like
a large wave, came rolling down the river, carrying with it numbers of
junks, boats, houses, trees, cattle, and I should be afraid to say how
many human beings, all mixed up in the most inextricable confusion.
We heard that the river Han had somewhere received an enormous and
sudden flood of water, which, added to its already swollen state, had for
many miles flooded the country, and was washing all before it into the
Yangtze. Across our anchor-chains eight or ten junks had drifted, and
were washed and piled up one over the other. It was impossible to reach
them to set them adrift, and I was very much afraid the extra strain on
the cables would be too much for them. Fortunately they held, thanks
to the best of iron, without a flaw in any of the links.

Numbers of junks came sweeping down with the flood, all unmanageable, many coming broadside on across our bows, which went
through them like a knife, the two parts of the junk floating past on
either side of our ship. It was quite impossible to launch a boat, she
would have been rolled over and swamped the moment she touched the
water. With great difficulty and with much risk, we managed to save the
lives of three or four dozen people; but, strange to say, some of them
were very much displeased at being fished up out of the water. The
Chinese said it was 'joss pidgeon', their fate, and as the river joss had
taken away their all, he had much better take themselves also. Three or
four afterwards tried to jump overboard. We put them ashore as soon
as we could, and so relieved ourselves of any further responsibility.'

William Spencer Percival, The Land of the Dragon: My Boating
and Shooting Excursions to the Gorges of the Upper Yangtse, 1889

HEADQUARTERS OF THE 1911 REVOLUTION
Known as the Red House, this building on Shouyi Lu was the headquarters of the 1911 Revolution against the Manchu Qing dynasty, led by Dr Sun Yatsen. Today, the building, in front of which stands a statue of Sun, is a museum to that revolution.

PEASANT MOVEMENT INSTITUTE MUSEUM
Mao Zedong directed this institute in the late 1920s. Its object was to train men to organize the peasants into associations to carry out underground activities.

EAST LAKE
A large scenic area, in the eastern suburbs of Wuchang, is centred on East Lake. Around its shores are numerous pavilions and halls, including a memorial to the Qu Yuan, the third-century BC poet (*see* page 76), and a monument to nine heroines who died fighting the Manchu troops during the Taiping Rebellion in the 19th century (*see* page 116). A low causeway leads to Moshan Hill and its botanical gardens with views across the city and the beautiful countryside.

DONGPO RED CLIFF
On the north bank of the Yangzi, just west of Huangzhou city, is the Red Cliff of Su Dongpo. On its summit are pavilions and halls dedicated to one of China's great poets, Su Dongpo (1037–1101). Having passed the imperial examinations at the young age of 20, he held various important scholarly posts in the Northern Song capital of Kaifeng but fell from grace when he criticized new law reforms. After arrest and imprisonment, he was demoted to the status of assistant commissioner to the Huangzhou militia. He lived in considerable hardship with his household of 20 members, tilling a few acres of land himself.

The Red Cliff became one of his favourite haunts, and he and his guests, boating beneath the cliff, would compose poetry, drink wine, admire the moon and carouse all night long. In the Qing dynasty (1644–1911) this cliff was named Dongpo Red Cliff to distinguish it from the other Red Cliff that was the scene of a battle in the Three Kingdoms period (*see* page 93). The Qing-dynasty halls contain examples of Su Dongpo's beautiful calligraphy, poems, essays and paintings carved on both stone and wooden tablets.

Qizhou

About one hour's sailing east of **Huangshi**, the industrial and iron ore mining city below Wuhan, is the small town of Qizhou. Though it has a history of 1,000 years, it is famous as the home town of Li Shizhen (1518–93), a Ming-dynasty herbalist and physician.

Flood level marker from 1931 on Customs House, Wuhan

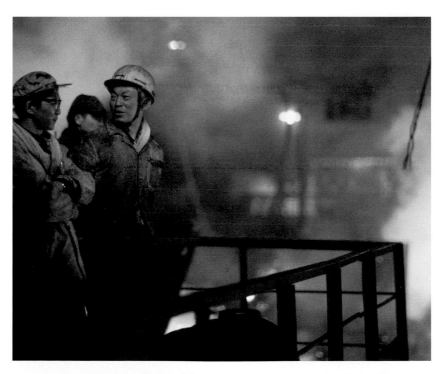

*The Wuhan steel mill, one of the country's largest, was constructed in 1957,
and employs over 120,000 workers*

OLD MAN RIVER: CHAIRMAN MAO AND THE YANGZI
—by Madeleine Lynn

All his life Chairman Mao loved swimming and regarded it as the best of sports, the struggle of man against nature. The Yangzi had powerful associations for him. He grew up with the stories of the heroic battles of the Three Kingdoms period (AD 220–65) which took place along the Yangzi and often sailed the river. His luxurious boat, the *Kunlun*, later became a tourist vessel. A constant theme in his writings is the overcoming of natural and man-made obstacles through sheer determination and courage. As he once observed: 'The Yangzi is a big river, people say. It is big, but not frightening. Is imperialist America big? We challenged it; nothing happened. So, there are things in this world that are big but not frightening.'

Naturally the idea of taming the Yangzi greatly appealed to him. In his 1956 poem 'Swimming', written about the Yangzi, he dreams of a great bridge and a dam to reshape the river forever:

> Great plans are afoot:
> A bridge will fly to span the north and south,
> Turning a deep chasm into a thoroughfare;
> Walls of stone will stand upstream to the west
> To hold back Wushan's clouds and rain
> Till a smooth lake rises in the narrow gorges.
> The mountain goddess if she is still there
> Will marvel at a world so changed.

He was referring to the bridge at Wuhan linking Hanyang and Wuchang, whose opening he presided at a few months later in 1957, naming it 'Iron and Steel Rainbow'. Mao expected that the Three Gorges dam would soon follow, but fierce controversy over the project delayed his dream until 1993, when work was finally begun. However, many still believe that the colossal project will never be completed (*see* page 62).

In 1956, 1958 and again most famously in 1966, Mao made a series of highly publicized long swims across the Yangzi at Wuhan (the above poem was written after the first of these). These were all years when Mao felt that his position was threatened by rumours of bad health and by the machinations of his enemies. Swimming the Yangzi was his way of showing the world that he was still healthy and in command; that he could keep his head above water, so to speak.

The celebrated 1966 swim, when Mao was 73, was part of the launch of the Cultural Revolution and the cult of Mao as a superhuman figure. Power struggles had been going on behind the scenes. Mao's whereabouts were kept secret and he had appeared in public only once all year. There were rumours that he was gravely ill or even dead. Then came the 16 July swim. Accompanying 5,000 young swimmers in the annual race across the river at Wuhan, he is reported to have swum almost 15 kilometres (9 miles) in 65 minutes, swimming along with the currents. Pictures of Mao's head bobbing above the water, surrounded by swimmers carrying huge banners celebrating his achievement, were seen not only throughout China but around the world. The message was clear; even in his 70s, Mao was a force to be reckoned with.

After practising Chinese medicine in his youth, Li spent 30 years rewriting and categorizing ancient Chinese medical books, travelling far and wide in search of specimens. His treatise formed 52 scrolls, with almost 2,000 entries. Sadly, he died before receiving recognition. However, his son presented a copy of Li's work to Emperor Wanli (1573–1620), a patron of scholarship. The emperor, much pleased with the work, ordered its wide distribution. Li Shizhen's classical works are the basis of traditional Chinese medical practice today and have been translated into a number of foreign languages.

The graves of Li Shizhen and his wife are situated at Rain Lake, north of the town, surrounded by gardens of medicinal herbs.

The local bamboo is used for making summer bed mats, and flutes made from this bamboo were widely praised as early as the Tang dynasty. Qizhou's White Flower Snake medicine is supposed to relieve rheumatic pains, while its Green Hairy-backed Turtles are used in medicines that allegedly cure tuberculosis and body fluid deficiencies.

About halfway between Qizhou and Jiujiang, the river leaves Hubei Province and thenceforth marks the provincial boundary between Hubei to the north and Jiangxi to the south as far as the mouth of Poyang Lake.

Jiujiang

Though the capital of Jiangxi Province is Nanchang, Jiujiang, with a population of 355,000, is the main port for distributing products from Poyang Lake and the surrounding counties as well as much of the chinaware produced at the porcelain capital of Jingdezhen. It has the reputation of being the hottest port on the Yangzi, with extremely oppressive summers. Though once an important tea-buying centre in its own right, it was gradually superseded by Wuhan, and tea grown in Jiangxi was shipped either upstream to Wuhan or downstream to Shanghai. Today, cotton textiles form Jiujiang's main industry.

Jiujiang is the main access city to one of China's most famous mountain beauty spots, Lushan, lying only a short distance to the south, which attracts 2.5 million tourists a year.

HISTORY OF JIUJIANG

In ancient times, nine rivers were said to have converged at this point, hence the name Jiujiang—'Nine Rivers'—though it was also called Jiangzhou and Xunyang. In its long history it has seen many upheavals; in the last century it was a Taiping stronghold from which the rebels held out against the imperial Qing armies for five years.

The area holds many memories for lovers of Chinese poetry. Tao Yuanming (365–429) lived at the foot of Lushan and was appointed magistrate of nearby Pengze County. This post was so poorly endowed that, rather than work 'for five pecks of grain to break one's back', he resigned after 83 days, preferring to eke out a living as a recluse in his home village. His essay *Peach Flower Garden* depicts his idea of a perfect society. Li Bai (701–62), implicated in the An Lushan Rebellion, was imprisoned briefly in Jiujiang in 757. Bai Juyi (772–846) also spent a period of official disgrace here as a middle-ranking official and is affectionately remembered. His poem *The Lute Song* tells of his sadness at his isolation in this small town. Su Dongpo was a frequent visitor to the area.

When Jiujiang was thrown open as a Treaty Port in 1861 it had suffered terribly as a consequence of the Taiping Rebellion (1850–64, *see* page 116). A British member of Lord Elgin's mission noted in 1858:

> We found it to the last degree deplorable. A single dilapidated street, composed only of a few mean shops, was all that existed of this once thriving and populous city: the remainder of the vast area, composed within walls five or six miles in circumference, contained nothing but ruins, weeds, and kitchen gardens.

Luding Bridge, an iron chained structure first erected in 1701, spans the Dadu River, a tributary of the upper Yangzi in Sichuan Province. It was stormed by the Red Army in June 1934

Jiujiang was once one of the three centres of the tea trade in China, along with Hankou and Fuzhou. There were two Russian factories producing brick-tea, but these ceased to operate after 1917. The British concession in Jiujiang was given up in 1927 after looting by mutineering garrisons and mobs.

WHAT TO SEE IN JIUJIANG

Sycamore trees line the streets of Jiujiang. The old down-town area is not large, sandwiched between Gantang Lake and the river bank. The old foreign concession area abuts the riversteamer dock and some old buildings remain—a church, the old French hospital and the Council House (now the Bank of China).

Crunchy, sweet Jiujiang tea biscuits made from tea oil, sesame and orange osmanthus flower originated in the Song dynasty; so did the potent, strange-tasting local wine, Fenggang Jiu, made from glutinous rice and fermented in sealed vats for five years.

■ GANTANG LAKE AND YANSHUI PAVILION

Gantang Lake is divided into two by a dike and bridge built in 821. The Sixian Bridge, now enlarged, still stands on the causeway which one crosses to reach Yangyue Pavilion on the low hill overlooking the lake. It is well stocked with silver and grass carp, and seagulls skim its surface. It is said that in the Three Kingdoms period (220–265) the Eastern Wu general, Zhou Yu, inspected his war ships from a reviewing platform on the lake, traces of which remain.

Linked to the shore by a zigzag bridge is the pretty **Yanshui (Misty Water) Pavilion**. A pavilion was first built here in the Tang dynasty (618–907) by the poet Bai Juyi during his unhappy posting in Jiujiang. It was named the Drenched Moon Pavilion after a line from one of his poems: 'Bidding farewell I saw the moon drenched by the river.'

In the Northern Song period (960–1127) a highly regarded Neo-Confucian philosopher, Zhou Dun, taught in Jiujiang and his son built a pavilion on the lake to his father's memory, calling it Yanshui Pavilion. The present island pavilion dates from the late Qing period (1644–1911). One small hall is dedicated to Bai Juyi, and other rooms display local archaeological discoveries. The city's antiques store is located here.

■ NENGREN TEMPLE

The Qing halls here are the oldest buildings left in Jiujiang, although the temple was established earlier, in the sixth century. Three or four monks and several nuns tend the temple. The seven-storey **Great Victory Pagoda**, beside the temple, dates from the Song period (960–1279).

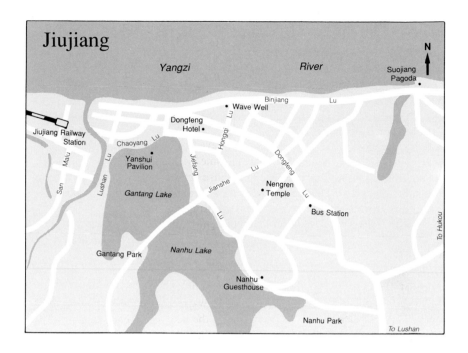

■ SUOJIANG PAGODA

This sexagonal seven-storey pagoda, overlooking the Yangzi embankment to the north-east of the city, was built in 1585. Damage to the 35-metre (115-foot) high pagoda caused by shelling from Japanese gunboats in World War II is still visible.

■ LANG JING (WAVE WELL)

In Yuliang Bei Lu near the waterfront is a small ancient well with a quaint history. Dug early in the Han dynasty (206 BC–AD 220), it connected with the Yangzi so that when a wind created waves on the river the surface of the well water would ripple too. The well became clogged and disused over the years until it was rediscovered in the third century, and the original inscription and date were uncovered. This was such a good omen that the well was renamed Auspicious Well. The poet Li Bai in the eighth century referred to it as the Wave Well in one of his poems, as did Su Dongpo. Waves no longer appear on its surface but the well is still in use.

■ DONGLIN MONASTERY

Twenty-two kilometres (13.5 miles) southwest of Jiujiang at the foot of Lushan is the

Donglin (Eastern Forest) Monastery, built in 386 for the monk Hui Yuan (334–416), founder of the Pure Land sect of Buddhism, whose overgrown grave is behind the temple. He spent many years translating Buddhist scriptures, and among his 123 disciples were an Indian and a Nepali. The monastery reached its zenith in the Tang dynasty (618–907), with a vast library of scriptures and over 300 halls and residences. Seriously damaged during the Taiping Rebellion (1850–64), the monastery was almost ruined in the Republican period (1911–49). Today there is a community of 20 monks who hold daily services in the temple halls. Behind the temple in a bamboo grove is the Well of Intelligence—from which every visitor is anxious for a sip. The Luohan Pine trees in the courtyard are said to have been planted by Hui Yuan himself. Hui Yuan is also said to have struck the ground with his staff, causing the Ancient Dragon Spring to gush forth, thus proving his right to establish himself here.

Nearby is the Xilin Pagoda, all that remains of an earlier monastery complex.

LUSHAN

Lushan, in the vicinity of Jiujiang, has always been appreciated by the Chinese as a mountain of great beauty and as a haven from the intense humid heat of the Yangzi valley summers. Its views eastwards to Poyang Lake and northward across the river are spectacular.

Since passengers from the downstream steamers usually disembark in the small hours of the morning, it is possible to enjoy the sunrise as your vehicle negotiates the hairpin bends on the 29-kilometre (18-mile) trip to the top of Lushan.

April and May are the best times to visit, when the hills are covered with wild azalea and peach blossoms, and there are many waterfalls. In the enervating months of June, July and August, the average temperature on Lushan is a comfortable 23°C (73°F), and during this peak season 25,000 tourists visit each day. In autumn the numbers drop off markedly and one is able to enjoy the changing autumnal colours of the trees at leisure, though the waterfalls dry up.

The town of **Guling** was established at the end of the 19th century by foreign traders and missionaries as a summer retreat for their families from as far away as Shanghai. They built over 100 summer bungalows and an American hospital (now the Lushan Guesthouse). They would be carried by sedan chair along the narrow path up the mountainside. Chiang Kai-shek's summer house—Meilu Villa—is still there, as is his library which now houses the **Lushan Museum**. Beside this is **Lushan People's Theatre** where in 1959 the Communist Party of China held its eighth plenary session, known later as the Lushan Conference, which resulted in the dismissal of the People's Liberation Army Commander-in-Chief, Peng Dehuai. The **Botanical Garden** was established in 1934; it has more than 4,000 kinds of flowers, trees and other plants.

Strange rock shapes, sheer peaks (the highest, Dahanyang is 1,543 metres, or 5,060 feet), steep cliffs, overhangs and caves, as well as a wide variety of lovely trees, are some of the splendours of Lushan. Its mystery is captured by Su Dong-po, who wrote:

It's a ridge when looked at face to face,
It's a peak when looked at sidewise;
It's always not the same when looked at from afar or near, when looked at from above or below.
You don't know what Lushan is really like,
Merely because you yourself are living in it.

Special Lushan dishes are the small Stone Fish from the Xilin River (best eaten in spring and autumn), Stone Ear (a black fungus), and Stone Chicken (a black-skinned frog found in the damp caves on Lushan, tasting rather like chicken and best eaten between June and September), as well as fish from Poyang Lake.

Lushan's Misty Cloud Green Tea (Yunwu Lu Cha), once sent as tribute to the emperors, should be sampled. The tea leaves are processed seven times to obtain their special fragrance.

Guesthouses and sanatoriums (over 1,000 of them) abound in the Guling valley.

STONE BELL HILL (SHIZHONG SHAN)

By taking a small vehicular ferry across the mouth of Poyang Lake to Hukou, one may climb the small, 50-metre (165-foot) high Stone Bell Hill, to which visitors have been coming for centuries. The hill overlooks the lake and the Yangzi River, and the meeting of the waters is clearly defined by an abrupt colour change. Mystery surrounds the strange bell-like sound that can be heard at Stone Bell Hill. There are three theories: that the hill is shaped like a bell and is hollow inside; that the rock, when struck, rings like a bell; or that the water, lapping into the nooks and crannies around the base, causes a bell-like sound. Su Dongpo made three special trips to try to solve the mystery, and having eventually settled on the last explanation, wrote an essay on the subject.

The present buildings date from the mid-19th century when the Taiping rebel commander Shi Dakai, choosing the mouth of the lake as a defensive position, built a stronghold on the hill, occupying it between 1853 and 1857. The Qing armies, miscalculating their enemy's strength, entered the lake in their war-junks, whereupon the Taipings stretched ropes across the lake mouth, dividing the Qing navy into two and routing them. The Qing general, Zeng Guofan, utterly humiliated, attempted to drown himself but was rescued by his retinue. The remains of the Taiping army stronghold can still be seen, and a pavilion on the hillside contains a stone tablet dedicated by Zeng Guofan to those who lost their lives in that battle (see page 116).

Peng Yulin, also a Qing general, later built a wonderful villa here with winding balconies, small ponds, carved pavilions and exquisite gardens. The lovely two-storeyed **Plum Flower Hall (Meihua Ting)** was erected in memory of the cultivated young woman he loved but could not marry. She died of a broken heart and he painted 11,000 pictures of plum flowers with her in mind.

This hill is also called the Lower Stone Bell Hill to distinguish it from the Upper Stone Bell Hill nearby. There is a delightful legend about the formation of these two small hills. The supreme Daoist (Taoist) deity, the Jade Emperor, instructed one of his officials to find two bells suitable for his palace. The official searched everywhere until he finally found two stone hills shaped like bells. He was delivering them to the palace when his carrying pole broke at the mouth of Poyang Lake; the stone hills fell to the ground and have remained there ever since.

Sailing junk in Sichuan (see Special Topic and sketches on pages 24–27)

DRAGON PALACE CAVE

Sixty-seven kilometres (42 miles) east of Jiujiang, this 1,700-metre (1,860-yard) long natural cave is in the scenic surroundings of **Dark Dragon Hill (Wulong Shan)**, in Pengze County, Jiangxi Province. This natural beauty spot comprises eight adjoining caverns with interior limestone formations resembling palace lanterns, dragon thrones, boats and other objects. One section is called the East Sea Dragon Palace after the classic 16th-century Chinese novel *Journey to the West* (sometimes known as *Monkey*). Coloured lighting heightens the effect.

POYANG LAKE

The surface area of China's largest freshwater lake is around 5,000 square kilometres (1,930 square miles), increasing in size during the flood season and shrinking in winter. Five rivers flow into the lake and eight counties border it. The Yangzi, Poyang Lake and the Gan River formed a link, via the Meiling Pass on the border between Jiangxi and Guangdong provinces, as far south as Guangzhou. From ancient times, this fertile region has been one of the 'rice-bowls' of China. The Poyang teems with fish, such as mandarin, anchovy and whitebait. It continues to fulfil its age-old function as a transport link for local produce—grain, tea, silk, bamboo, and particularly the porcelain from the kaolin (white clay) potteries of Jingdezhen, which have been producing since the second century BC, and supplying the imperial court from the fifth century on.

A 22,000-hectare (54,000-acre) nature reserve has been established in the vicinity of Wucheng on the western side of the lake. It hosts Asia's greatest bird spectacle in winter, when over 4,000 cranes, 40,000 swan geese and around a quarter of a million ducks flock here. Over 90 per cent of the world's population of the Siberian Crane winter at the reserve. Numbers have increased dramatically since the area became a protected reserve, with 1,700 birds counted in 1988.

Owing to the lake's strategic importance, numerous naval encounters took place on its waters. Emperor Wudi (reigned 420–23) was embattled here. It was the site of a decisive battle in the overthrow of the Yuan dynasty in the 14th century. Another naval battle was fought between the Taiping rebels and the Qing imperial forces in 1855. Today, only graceful fishing boats in full sail occupy the lake.

Local fairy tales connect a small island in the lake, **Shoe Hill** or **Dagu Shan**, with the stories of Xiaogu Shan (*see* page 120) further downstream. It seems that Xiaogu Niang Niang and her betrothed escaped from her Emei Shan prison with the help of a precious umbrella. The pursuing Immortal, confronting them at Poyang Lake, threw his flying sword at the precious umbrella and, in her confusion, Xiaogu Niang Niang lost one of her embroidered slippers, which fell into the lake and was transformed into a shoe-shaped island.

THE TAIPING REBELLION —by Madeleine Lynn

There were many violent peasant uprisings between 1840–1911. But the Taiping Rebellion (1850–64) was more than just another revolt; it was the most devastating civil war the world has ever known. It affected nearly two-thirds of China, destroying entire cities and causing an estimated 20 to 30 million deaths, more people than China lost in the war against Japan (1937–45). A 1950s government census found that the population of provinces near the mouth of the Yangzi was still a total of 20 million lower than it had been in 1850.

The rebellions of the period were prompted by a series of interlinked misfortunes. The unpopular Manchurian Qing dynasty (1644–1911) was growing weaker and Western incursions more far-reaching. Thousands lost their jobs as traditional industries such as weaving were wiped out by Western imports. Corrupt officials taxed the peasants ever more extortionately in order to pay for these imports, the chief of which was opium. To make matters worse, untold numbers died in famine after terrible famine. These were caused by natural disasters, a huge population increase during the early Qing, and neglect of the irrigation systems.

The Taiping leader Hong Xiuquan was a poor school teacher from a village near Guangzhou (Canton) who had had some contact with missionaries and their teachings. After failing the imperial examinations several times, he suffered a nervous breakdown, during which he saw visions. These revealed to him that he was the son of God, the younger brother of Jesus Christ. His earthly mission was to expel the Manchu demons from China and to create a Heavenly Kingdom of Peace on earth (Taiping Tianguo), where all men and women would be equal.

The Taipings formally declared rebellion in 1851 and thousands of peasants and dispossessed workers rose up to join them. In 1852 they took to the water on a motley collection of boats and rafts, sweeping through the waterways of Guangxi, along the Grand Canal and up the Yangzi, sacking cities and amassing loot, boats and followers as they went. Their numbers grew to over a million people and they easily defeated the demoralized imperial troops in their path. In 1853 they reached Nanjing, where they set up their capital. From here they ruled over their Heavenly Kingdom for the next 11 years. At their peak, almost half of China was under their control.

After establishing their government, the Taipings sent an army to attack the Manchu capital of Beijing. But they were turned back by imperial forces organized by the big Northern landlords. Returning to Nanjing, they consolidated their power, successfully repelling a Qing attack in 1860 and to many it seemed that they would become the next ruling Dynasty.

Although it is hard to know how far the Taiping reforms extended throughout their territory, in Nanjing and its environs at least, land was divided equally between all men and women over 16, half-shares going to those under 16. Foot-binding, slavery and concubinage were abolished. Women served in their own battalions, which were commanded by female officers. Opium and infanticide were illegal.

Yet this supposedly egalitarian society was actually a totalitarian theocracy, run by the Heavenly King Hong Xiuquan himself and four assistant Kings. While ordinary Taipings were allowed only one wife and lived spartan, disciplined lives, the Kings lived in luxury surrounded by concubines. As time went on Hong became ever more paranoid and in 1856, suspecting the East King of treachery, he had him and about 20,000 of his followers killed in one bloody night. Later he also turned on the North King and had him assassinated.

Meanwhile after the defeat of 1860, the Manchus and Chinese gentry continued to fight the Taipings under the able leadership of Zeng Guofan. At first the Western powers remained neutral and many Westerners, particularly missionaries, were favourable towards the Taipings. But the devastation they wrought—some cities changed hands so many times in the fighting that there was little left to fight over—and a closer look at their version of Christianity, changed most people's minds. The final straw came when the Taipings closed in on Shanghai in 1862 and threatened the foreign community there. Thereafter the West supplied the Manchus with western weapons and lent them commanders to train their forces. One such was 'Chinese Gordon', who took part in the burning of the Summer Palace and later died at Khartoum.

The end came with the long siege of Nanjing in 1864. As the siege wore on, Hong grew more and more out of touch with reality. After praying for Manna from Heaven, he told his starving citizens to gather ten loads each of grass and leaves and eat that. A few days before the imperial forces finally dynamited the city walls, he committed suicide by swallowing gold mixed with wine. Not one Taiping surrendered. Many committed suicide, chanting hymns as they did so, some by throwing themselves in the moat, others by torching their houses. Many of Hong's concubines hanged themselves in the Palace garden. Over 7,000 people were massacred in three days. Lord Elgin on visiting Nanjing soon afterwards, said that the desertion of the streets and the universal stillness reminded him of Pompeii.

The Lower Reaches:
Hukou to the Yellow Sea

The region around the lower Yangzi and its delta, the most prosperous in the country, is known as China's 'Land of Fish and Rice'.

From Hukou at the mouth of the Poyang, the Yangzi widens on its final sweep to the Yellow Sea, skirting northern Jiangxi and traversing the provinces of Anhui and Jiangsu. Hundreds of shallow lakes and streams, rich in freshwater crabs, prawns and fish, feed the river. From Nanjing downwards the river becomes tidal, and ocean-going vessels of 10,000 to 15,000 tons navigate its channels.

The deltaic plain of coastal Jiangsu—the most densely populated of China's provinces—is a veritable maze of natural waterways, man-made dikes and canals. Mulberry trees line their banks and humpbacked stone bridges link the picturesque towns and villages. These waterways serve as irrigation channels, drainage outlets and transport canals. Three staple grain crops—two of paddy rice and one of winter wheat—are harvested each year. Since earliest times, sericulture has been an important economic factor, and though cotton replaced silk in importance after the 1930s, silkworm breeding is still a major home industry and hard-cash earner for peasant families. Sericulture formed the basis on which the region's famous textile cities of Hangzhou, Suzhou, Wuxi, Nanjing and Shanghai were established.

Water conservation plans are underway to divert water from the Yangzi northwards, linking up with similar projects on the Huai River, which will eventually irrigate the large arid areas of north China.

Neolithic rice-growing cultures occupied this area as early as 5000 BC, domesticating pigs and dogs. By the fifth century BC much of the lower Yangzi formed one of nine huge provincial areas known as Yangzhou; its imperial tribute included silks, fruits and timber. During the Tang dynasty (618–907) the city of Yangzhou was the main port of call for Arabian traders.

The town of Jiangyin demarcates the estuary, and for the next 200 kilometres (125 miles) the Yangzi widens from 1,200 metres (1,300 yards) to 91 kilometres (56 miles) below the confluence with the Huangpu, the last of its tributaries. In ancient times the Yangzi was said to have had three mouths; down the centuries the river outlet was a source of much academic speculation in China, as silt deposits continually changed the shape and form of the river's mouth. Now its outlet to the Yellow Sea is divided into two by the intensely cultivated island of Chongming (1,083 square kilometres, or 420 square miles, in area) and by several smaller islands, whose farming produce supplies the massive Shanghai area (*see* satellite photograph on page 4–5). In August 1983, when low-lying land in

A large junk under full sail, a rare sight on the Yangzi River today

30 Anhui counties that border the Yangzi was inundated by flood waters, nearly a million peasants battled to drain the land and sow autumn crops. Ninety people were reported dead and hundreds injured as the flood crest swept by. In Jiangsu, 500,000 civilians and soldiers reinforced dikes and stood watch as floods threatened Nanjing and other cities along the banks. Luckily no further serious damage occurred.

XIAOGU SHAN

About 35 kilometres (22 miles) below the mouth of the Poyang, the magical little island of Xiaogu Shan comes into view. It is situated by the north bank of the Yangzi in Anhui Province, while across the river is the county town of Pengze in Jiangxi.

The white walls and grey-tile roofs of Qisu Monastery nestle into Xiaogu Shan's steep slope, and pavilions adorn its bamboo-groved peak. A handful of elderly monks inhabit the temple (first established in the Song dynasty, 907–1279), which is dedicated to Xiaogu Niang Niang, and visited by childless women offering incense to her.

As a result of silt accumulation, Xiaogu Shan now adjoins the riverbank. The characters 'First Pass of the Sea Gate' are painted on the rock face. Stairs lead up to the monastery, but to reach the peak one must cling to chains fixed to the rock to negotiate the steep climb.

The island is named after the legendary Lin Xiaogu, later known as Xiaogu Niang Niang, who grew up in Fujian Province and became betrothed to a local village lad, Peng Liang. Unhappily, her parents died, and she was adopted by a Daoist (Taoist) Immortal at Mount Emei in Sichuan Province, where she studied Daoism for many years. One day, while gathering herbs on the mountain, she slipped and fell, and was saved by a wandering woodcutter who was none other than Peng Liang. Peng's mother, attending to the girl's injuries, noticed a small birthmark behind her ear and recognized her as the long-lost Lin Xiaogu. In renewing her betrothal to Peng Liang, Xiaogu broke her religious vows and was incarcerated by the Immortal.

With the help of a sympathetic monk she stole the Immortal's precious umbrella, and the lovers flew away. However, the pursuing Immortal cut off their escape at Poyang Lake with his flying sword, which tore the umbrella and caused Xiaogu to drop her slipper (see page 115). At Pengze the umbrella finally split in two. The lovers fell on different sides of the Yangzi, turning into two steep hills: Pengliang Ji on the south and Xiaogu Shan on the north. The temple on Pengliang Ji was destroyed in the Cultural Revolution (1966–76).

At the top of Xiaogu Shan is her 'Make-up and Dressing Terrace'. A stone tablet beside it describes her story, as well as a related anecdote concerning Zhu Yuanzhong, founder of the Ming dynasty in 1368, who was saved by the appearance of Xiaogu Niang Niang while retreating downstream one night after a naval defeat.

About 32 kilometres (20 miles) below Pengze the river enters Anhui and winds its way northeast across the province until, just below Ma'anshan, it enters the province of Jiangsu. Bulk carriers, strings of barges and fishing *sampans*—their nets attached to long bamboo poles extending forward and aft—frequent the stretch of river between here and Anqing, about three hours' sailing downriver. The south bank is hilly while the north bank is flat, broken only by trees and bamboo groves. A number of shallow lakes feed into the river.

Anqing

The city of Anqing, on the north bank, is situated in that area of Anhui Province called Huainan, meaning south of the Huai River. It is built along the Dalong Hills amidst pretty surroundings. Historical records refer to the appointment of an official to the town as early as the Spring and Autumn period (770–476 BC). During the Qing dynasty (1644–1911) and the Republican period (1911–49) the city was the capital of the province, though today the capital is Hefei, further north. Anqing's main function is to gather and distribute local produce; it also has a petrochemical industry.

The handsome octagonal **Zhenfeng Pagoda**, the major landmark, was built in 1570 amidst the remains of the Song-dynasty Welcoming the River Temple (Yingjiang Si). A fine view of the city can be enjoyed from its top storey.

The pagoda was built by a Daoist (Taoist) architect, Zhang Wencai, who was brought to Anqing specially from Baiyun Temple in Beijing. Stone balconies surround six of its seven storeys. Inside, over 600 Buddha images cover the brick walls. Set into the lower half of the pagoda are images of the local prefect, Wang Erquan, who commissioned its construction, and other personages of the period.

The town was occupied by the Taiping rebels for six years, and one of its kings built a residence here (*see* page 116). It seems that the imperial defences of Anqing left much to be desired, for when it fell to the rebels in 1853 Emperor Xianfeng wrote: 'Great has been my indignation on reading the memorial . . . how could that important provincial capital be captured by the bandits in one day?' The city, retaken in 1861, was ravaged. Travellers to the city 60 years later noted that large parts of it were still in ruins.

Riverboats stop at **Guichi** (at the mouth of the Qiupu River), which is the closest Yangzi port for those visiting the sacred Buddhist mountain of Jiuhua and the famous scenic area of Huangshan to the south. Though transport facilities to these sites are being developed at Guichi, the city of Wuhu, further downriver, offers more.

Economy of Time and Labour, *copper engraving, c. 1790*

Chinese Junk, *gouache on pith paper, 19th century*

Wuhu

Wuhu, on the south bank of the river, is in southeastern Anhui Province at the confluence of the Qingyi and Yangzi Rivers. Its population is only 440,000, not large by Chinese standards. In the last century, Wuhu was one of the four great rice-marketing centres (the others being Wuxi, Jiujiang and Changsha), but it is now principally a producer of light-industrial goods, such as thermos flasks, machine tools, cotton textiles, kitschy mantlepiece clocks and cement. It is specially known for its scissors, its variety of local twig and leaf brooms and its wrought-iron pictures.

As a good transportation system links Wuhu with other parts of the province, the city is a transfer stop for visitors to the famous scenic spots of Huangshan and Jiuhua.

HISTORY OF WUHU

In the Spring and Autumn period (770–476 BC) the city was known as Jiuzi. Its present name was adopted in the Han dynasty (206 BC–AD 220). By the Three Kingdoms period (220–65 AD, *see* page 42) it had become a strategically important town in the Kingdom of Eastern Wu. In a fierce battle between the Kingdoms of Eastern Wu and Shu, the Wu general Zhou Yu was killed. The King of Wu, Sun Quan, donned white mourning clothes and made a special journey to Wuhu to receive Zhou Yu's coffin.

In the Tang dynasty (618–907) the poet Du Fu's many visits were recollected in his poem, *Thoughts on Staying Again at Wuhu*. When Wuhu became a Treaty Port under the Chefoo Convention of 1876 a small foreign community resided here. Trading principally in rice, wood and tea, it had become a flourishing commercial port by the end of the 19th century. Trade dropped off severely in the 1920s and 1930s due to bandit activity in the area.

WHAT TO SEE IN WUHU

There is little of historical interest to be found in Wuhu, but a stroll along the east embankment of the Qingyi River is worthwhile. Here barges and small boats load and discharge vegetables, fruit, sand and everyday items; boat families and their pets add to the cacophony of noise. Bamboo rafts, at intervals along the river's edge, serve as platforms for the local women to do their washing. In the narrow streets parallel to the river, such as Zhongchang Jie and Shangchang Jie, shops sell fishing tackle and nets, baskets, firecrackers, bamboo steamers, and Chinese weights and measures. In the cobbled streets, bamboo chicken coops stand outside front doors that open into dark, high-ceilinged old houses. Xinwu Jie running west off the main street, Zhongshan Jie, is busy with restaurants and food stalls serving crispy rice cakes, sweet dumpling soup and large dough fritters. Near the scruffy memorial to the 1949

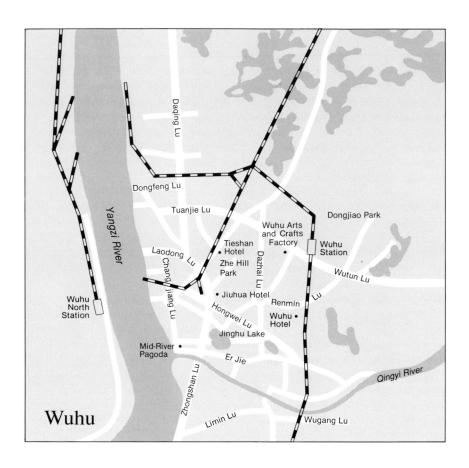

Wuhu

Revolution is Jiuhe Jie, which is now a market area. At No. 26 a huge, fanciful, American-built Catholic Church, dating from the Treaty Port days, is open for worship on Sundays. At Jinghu Lake, in the town centre, people gather to play cards or chess and to sell their miniature potted plants.

■ ZHE HILL

The highest point in the city is only 86 metres (282 feet), but the view from the pagoda at the top sweeps over the whole city and down the Yangzi. It seems that this five-storey **Zheshan Pagoda** and the Mid-River Pagoda (see below) were built at the same time, at the beginning of the Song dynasty (960–1279). A competition apparently developed between the two teams of builders. The two brothers engaged on the construction of Zheshan Pagoda, who were desperate to complete first and so avoid losing face, finished off the very top with a cooking wok turned upside down. A small zoo is to be found in the public park.

■ GUANGJI TEMPLE
Of the four main temples which existed in Wuhu, three were destroyed in the Sino-Japanese War and only the Guangji Temple, at the foot of Zhe Hill, remains. The main hall is hung with ten scrolls depicting the Buddhist Hell. The monastery was established in the Tang dynasty (618–907) and Emperor Dezong (reigned 780–5) came here as a monk. When omens indicated that this was an unsafe place for him to reside, he went to live on the famous Buddhist mountain of Jiuhua, further south.

■ MID-RIVER PAGODA
This six-storey pagoda stands at the point where the Qingyi River enters the Yangzi, a danger spot for navigation. A local fisherman named Huang suggested that this octagonal pagoda be built to serve as a lighthouse. Its name derives from its position—it is exactly in the middle of the lower reaches of the Yangzi.

■ WUHU ARTS AND CRAFTS FACTORY
The art of wrought-iron picture-making originated in Wuhu and this factory in Jiuhua Lu continues the tradition, besides producing pictures made of feathers or golden wheat stalks, poker-burned wooden decorations and copies of old paintings.
Iron picture-making is very laborious and amazingly intricate. This art form was started by an itinerant blacksmith, Tang Tianchi, during the reign of Emperor Kangxi (1662–1723). Tang used to sit and watch a local painter, whose work he much admired. The artist chided Tang: 'I paint my pictures, you beat your iron, but you will never make pictures by beating iron.' Tang promptly went away and produced an iron picture, 'using a hammer as a brush and iron as ink'.
A huge 'Welcoming Pine' iron picture by the artists of Wuhu adorns the Anhui Room in the Great Hall of the People in Beijing.

Ma'anshan

Anhui's biggest industrial city, Ma'anshan, mines much of the pig iron used in the Shanghai steel industry. It also has its own iron and steel works, limestone quarries, and chemical and cement factories. The city is linked to Wuhu and Nanjing by rail.
A touching story is told of the city's name, which means Horse Saddle Hill. When the Kingdoms of Chu and Shu were at war in the third century, General Xiang Yu of Chu was defeated by Liu Bei and attempted to retreat to Wujiang on the north bank

of the Yangzi. Finding only a small boat, he had his precious mount ferried across first. At this moment Liu Bei's pursuing soldiers arrived and Xiang Yu, knowing he was trapped, cut his throat with his own sword. Seeing his master's courageous suicide, the horse leapt into the river and drowned. The boatman buried its saddle on the nearby hill.

Buildings on **Coloured Stone Cliff (Caishi Ji)**, west of the city, commemorate the Tang poet, Li Bai (701–62). The three-storeyed Taibai Lou houses two Chinese boxwood statues of the poet, one depicting his immortal gesture of inviting the moon to join him in a cup of wine. Here too is the 'Tomb of Li Bai's Clothes and Official Hat'. According to the local legend, Li Bai's clothing was buried on Caishi Ji when he drowned after falling drunkenly from a boat one evening while attempting to embrace the moon's reflection in the river.

The **Three Scholars Grotto (Sanyuan Dong)** was allegedly built by three grateful gentlemen who, on their way to the capital to take the imperial examinations, found safety and shelter under the cliff when their boat was caught in a sudden and violent storm. After all three had gained first-class honours and promotions, they recalled their close shave and donated funds for the building of this grotto.

Nanjing

Nanjing—'Southern Capital'—along with Luoyang, Xi'an and Beijing, is one of the historical capitals of China, and the many imperial tombs and architectural remains in the city and its environs reflect its grandiose past. Today, the city is the capital of Jiangsu Province, with a population of some 4.5 million. Its industries include machine-building, automobile assembly, electronics, petroleum, iron and steel, textiles, shipbuilding and foodstuffs. A double-tiered road and rail bridge, completed in 1968, spans the Yangzi at Nanjing.

HISTORY OF NANJING
With the Yangzi on one side, and surrounded on the other three sides by hills, Nanjing was thought to be auspicious as well as strategically important. First historical records date from the Spring and Autumn period (770–476 BC) when the area was divided between the Kingdoms of Wu, Yue and Chu. A walled town was built during the Eastern Han period (AD 25–220), known as 'Stone City'.

Between the third and fourteenth centuries, eight dynasties established their capitals in the city, some of them building magnificent palaces and forts. Though many of these minor dynasties had incompetent rulers and regimes weakened by intrigue and debauchery, Nanjing emerged as a cultural centre of painting, philoophy and Buddhism. In the sixth century, the Sui dynasty established its capital at

Nanjing

ZIJINSHAN (PURPLE AND GOLD MOUNTAINS)

Legend:
★ Hotel
∏ Gate
— Ming-dynasty wall
— Cable Car

© The Guidebook Company Ltd

0   500   1000   1500 m
0   500   1000   1500 yds

N ←

Places / labels:
Beamless Hill
Tablet of Three Marvels
Lingou Monastery
Sun Zhongshan (Sun Yat-sen) Mausoleum
Ming Tomb
Zhongshan Botanical Gardens
First Peak 448m
Observatory
Pipa Lake
Qixia Lake
Zhongshan Gate
Moat
Jiangsu Museum
Ruins of Ming Palace
Wuchao Gate
Taiping Gate
Fugui Hill
Jiuhua Hill
Houzaimen Jie
Zhou Enlai's House
Plum Garden Village
Sichuan Restaurant
Renmin Theatre
Xuanwu Park
Xuanwu Lake
Zoo
Jiefang Gate
Xuanwu Gate
Hospital
Jiangsu Restaurant
Tiatung Museum
Confucius Temple
Nanjing People's Hall
Telegraph Office
Jinhrici Building
Bank of China
Dasanyuan Restaurant
Cockcrow Temple
Arts & Crafts Shop
Bell Tower
Drum Tower
Nanjing Railway Station
Nanjing Bus Terminal
Xuanwu Hotel
Maxiangong Muslim Restaurant
Ticket Office for Railway, Highway & Waterway
Jinling Hotel
Central Hotel
Wutaishan Gymnasium
Tongqingou Restaurant
Heaven Worshipping Palace
Nanjing Teachers' College
Hongqiao Hotel
Overseas Chinese Hotel
CITS
Nanjing Hotel
Zhongshan Hotel
Dingshan Hotel
Shuangmenlou Hotel
Dinghui Gate
Gulin Park
Qingliangshan Stone Citadel
Hospital
Mochou Park
Mochou Lake
Naohu Lake
Loto Hill
Xiuqiu Park
Yijiang Gate
Zhongshan Wharf
Anti-Japanese War Museum and Memorial to Nanjing Massacre

Roads / rivers:
BEIJING - SHANGHAI RAILWAY
Ninghai Highway
Kexuejishi Lu
Longpan Lu
Heyan Highway
Taipingmen Lu
Minglinglu Lu
Minglinglu Lu
Xuanwujin Lu
Ninghai Highway
Xiaoying Lu
Beijing Dong Lu
Beijing Dong Lu
Zhongshan Dong Lu
Dagiaolu Lu
Yudao Jie
Zhujiang Lu
Zhongyang Lu
Hunan Lu
Bei Lu
Xinmofan Lu
Jiangsu Lu
Beijing Xi Lu
Ninghai Lu
Zhongshan Lu
Zhongshan Nan Lu
Taiping Nan Lu
Shengzhou Lu
Guangzhou Lu
Hanzhong Lu
Mochou Lu
Hanzhong Lu
Hanzhong Lu
Guangzhou Lu
Hujunan Lu
Fengtai Lu
Shuiximen Lu
Changdong Lu
Shuimugangwai Dajie
Challong Dong Jie
Qinhuai River
Hujuhu Lu
Gulou Lu
Jiangning Lu
Hangkou Lu
Huju Bei Lu
Huju Nan Lu
Rehe Lu
Rehe Nan Lu
Daqiao Nan Lu
Jinchuan River
Chenghe Lu
ZHONGYANGMEN
GUANGHUAMEN
SHUIXIMEN
HANZHONGMEN
JIANGDONGMEN
to Qixia Monastery
Chalukou
to Airport
to Yangtze Bridge
Ferries to Shanghai & Wuhan
Yangzi River
Qinhuai River

128

Xi'an, and ordered the complete destruction of earlier dynastic buildings in Nanjing.
The city flourished again during the Tang dynasty (618–907), when the great poets Li Bai, Bai Juyi and Liu Yuxi lived here for a while. For a brief period, Nanjing (then called Jinling) became the capital of the Southern Song, but the dynastic base had to be moved to Hangzhou as the pursuing Nuzhen Tartar armies advanced. Marco Polo visited the city in 1275.

The founder of the Ming dynasty, Zhu Yuanzhang, captured Nanjing in 1356 and set up his capital here, building palaces, temples and pagodas. (The famous green- and white-glazed-tile Porcelain Pagoda of the Baoen Temple, so often praised as one of the seven wonders of the world by earlier travellers, belonged to this period, though it was totally destroyed during the Taiping Rebellion (1850–64). Some of its tiles are on exhibition at the Chaotian Gong.) He also enlarged the city wall to make it the longest in the world. Earlier Tang-dynasty poets had written lyrically of being entertained on 'singsong boats'—sort of floating bordellos—along the Qinhuai (a 10-kilometre, or 6-mile, man-made river, said to have been dug during the second century BC, skirting the western and southern edges of Nanjing). A picture of more innocent pleasures is conjured up by a passage from *The Scholars*, an early 18th-century novel by Wu Ching-tzu:

> After the middle of the fourth month in Nanking, the Chin-huai River becomes quite lovely. The barges from other tributaries of the Yangtze dismantle their cabins, set up awnings, and paddle into the river. Each vessel carries a small, square, gilt-lacquered table, set with an Yihsing stoneware pot, cups of the finest Cheng Hua or Hsuan Te porcelain, and the choicest tea brewed with rain water. Boating parties bring wine, dishes and sweetmeats with them to the canal, and even people travelling by boat order a few cents' worth of good tea to drink on board as they proceed slowly on their way. At dusk two bright horn lanterns on each vessel are reflected in the water as the barges ply to and fro, so that above and below are bright. Fluting and singing are heard all night and every night from Literary Virtue Bridge to Lucky Crossing Bridge and East Water Guardhouse. The pleasure-goers buy water-rat fireworks too, which project from the water and look like pear trees in blossom when let off. The fun goes on till the fourth watch each night.

Translated by Yang Hsien-yi and Gladys Yang

During the Ming dynasty (1368–1644), an imperial decree established a special government department to oversee brothels which catered to the 200,000 garrisoned troops in the city. The capital was moved to Beijing in 1420, but Nanjing remained a subsidiary capital and financial centre.

In the Qing dynasty (1644–1911) troops were garrisoned in the city. The Treaty of Nanking ending the Opium War of 1842 was signed aboard *HMS*

Cornwallis between the British and the Chinese. It ceded the territory of Hong Kong to Britain, opened four Chinese ports to foreign trade, and exacted the payment of 21 million Mexican dollars as indemnity from the Chinese. It was the first of what became known as the Unequal Treaties. The pseudo-Christian Taiping Rebellion made its headquarters in Nanjing in 1853 and occupied it for 11 years (*see* page 116). Its leader, Hong Xiuquan, adopted the title 'Heavenly King' and appointed other leaders as Princes of the East, West, North and South'. The 'Heavenly King' built a palace of thousands of rooms of which little now remains. The city was almost completely destroyed in the devastation and killings that followed the overthrow of this rebellion. Nanjing became a Treaty Port under the terms of the Franco-Chinese Treaty of 1897.

Following the revolution of 1911, Nanjing was declared the capital of the Republic of China in 1912. (Dr Sun Yatsen, founder of the Nationalist Republic, was buried here in 1929.) The Nationalists regained control over Nanjing from the local warlord in 1926, and it remained the capital until just before the Japanese occupation of the city in 1937, when an estimated 400,000 residents perished in what became known as the 'Rape of Nanjing'. In early 1949 the People's Liberation Army entered Nanjing, driving the Nationalist government before it, first to Guangzhou and then to Taiwan.

WHAT TO SEE IN NANJING

Nanjing's streets are lined with poplars and sycamore trees —some of which came from France—that provide some relief from the oppressive summer temperatures. Gardens and parks add grace and a sense of spaciousness to the city. Two lakes, **Xuanwu Lake** and **Mochou Lake**, are surrounded by parkland. Many of the historical relics—tombs, stelae and sculptures dating from the sixth century—are to be found in the hills and fields around Nanjing, the best known in the vicinity of Zijinshan (Purple and Gold Mountain).

SIGHTS WITHIN THE CITY

■ ZHONGHUAMEN GATE AND MING-DYNASTY CITY WALL

Built by the first Ming emperor, Hongwu, this wall of clay bricks took 20 years to construct (1366–86), and included remains of an earlier Eastern Han city wall (Stone City). It encloses an area of 41 square kilometres (16 square miles), making it the longest city wall in the world. Its highest point is 18 metres (60 feet), and it varies in width from 7 to 12 metres (30 to 40 feet). Some 200,000 workers cemented the bricks—each stamped with details of the brickmaker and overseer—with a mortar mixture of glutinous rice, tung oil and lime.

The impressive Zhonghuamen Gate in the southern part of the city has four vaulted gates and was probably garrisoned by troops; along with the **Hepingmen Gate**, these are all that remain of 13 original Ming gates that were largely destroyed

(following pages) The Yangzi River Bridge, Nanjing

in the Taiping Rebellion (1850–64). Other gates have been built in the 20th century to facilitate traffic flow.

■ THE DRUM TOWER (GU LOU) AND BELL PAVILION (DAZHONG TING),
ZHONGSHAN BEI LU

The Drum Tower marks the centre of Nanjing. It was built in 1382, and was followed in 1388 by the Bell Pavilion, to the northeast. Both were used to sound out the two-hourly night watches over the city. The Drum Tower is a Qing-dynasty (1644–1911) reconstruction built over the 14th-century Ming foundations. A tearoom at the top offers a fine view of the city. The hexagonal Bell Pavilion, also originally erected in the Ming dynasty, houses a huge one-ton bronze bell and a memorial hall. The hall is dedicated to the two daughters of the artisan who was ordered by the emperor to cast the bell. Legend tells how, after the craftsman had made several unsuccessful attempts to produce a correct blend of metals for the bronze, the two girls threw themselves into the smelter, whereupon the composition of the alloy was miraculously perfected. As a result of this filial sacrifice, he was literally saved by the bell from certain execution. The existing two-storeyed pavilion dates from 1889.

■ YANGZI RIVER BRIDGE (CHANGJIANG DAQIAO)

The waters of the Yangzi become tidal at Nanjing. Astride the swirling current stands the Great Changjiang Bridge. The visitor is proudly shown this city landmark, which provides a vital link between the north of China and the fertile fields of Jiangnan. Before the bridge was completed in 1968, all traffic had to cross the river by ferry.

Initially the bridge was to be constructed with the help of the Russians, who agreed to supply the design, technical expertise and steel. When deteriorating Sino-Soviet relations led to the Russians' withdrawal in 1960, the Chinese not only constructed the bridge themselves but revamped the domestic steel industry to produce the necessary tonnage. The project took them eight years.

At either end of the bridge stand four towers. In one of these is housed the visitors' briefing room and a fine model of the Yangzi Bridge. The bridge, 1.6 kilometres (1 mile) long, is two-tiered, with the top level for vehicles and the lower one for trains. A visit to the railway deck to look along the great grey tunnel of steel is awe-inspiring, especially if a train thunders past.

■ JIANGSU PROVINCIAL MUSEUM, 321 EAST ZHONGSHAN LU

The 400,000 cultural relics here date from around the 11th century BC up to the founding of the People's Republic. Exhibits include jade, pottery and stone implements from Jiangsu's prehistoric period; artifacts from the Longshan and associated cultures from 4000 to 2500 BC; and a wide range of porcelain, paintings, and bronzes, as well as maps and displays of traditional handicrafts. The famous jade burial suit, exhibited abroad in the 1970s, belongs to this museum. It is thought to be 1,800 years old and is made of 2,600 rectangles of jade sewn together with silver thread. The jade suit was made to totally encapsulate the body with the object of preserving it, but when archaeologists dug it up in Xuzhou in 1970 all they discovered inside were bones.

One of the most fascinating exhibits is the large wooden copy of a statue of a man showing all the body's acupuncture points. The original bronze statue is believed to date from the Warring States period (475–221 BC). Another reminder of China's superiority in early medical pioneering is a portrait of Hua Tuo (141–203), who practised acupuncture and surgery and reputedly employed anaesthetics 1,000 years before they were discovered in the West.

■ RUINS OF THE MING IMPERIAL PALACE
Nearby, on Yudao Jie near Wuchao Gate, is the site of the palace built by the first Ming emperor, Hongwu (reigned 1368–98). It was destroyed in 1645 and all that remains are some foundation stones, stone lions and the stone screen wall facing the former palace.

■ MUSEUM OF THE TAIPING HEAVENLY KINGDOM, ZHANYUAN LU
Housed in the remains of the former palace of the Eastern Prince of the Heavenly Kingdom is a detailed exhibition of maps, paintings, documents and other relics of the Taiping Rebellion (see page 116). Many of the documents are copies, as the originals are held in Beijing. Linked to the museum is the charming Zhan Yuan, a traditional Chinese garden which originated in the early Ming dynasty and eventually became incorporated into the palace of the Eastern Prince, Yang Xiuqing, in the 19th century.

■ PLUM GARDEN VILLAGE (MEIYUAN XINCUN)
At the end of the Sino-Japanese War, abortive peace talks took place between the Guomindang and the Communist Party of China. During this period—May 1946 to March 1947—the communists made their headquarters at 17, 30 and 31 Meiyuan Xincun, a suburb close to the centre of Nanjing.

The communist delegation was led by Zhou Enlai and Dong Biwu. Zhou Enlai and his wife, Deng Yingchao, lived at No. 30, and the charming house and garden remain just as the couple left them, with jackets hanging from a hatstand and a battered leather briefcase on the chest of drawers in the spartan bedroom. A doorway knocked into the eastern garden wall connects No. 30 to No. 31; this short cut enabled the communists to evade constant surveillance by Guomindang secret agents

Bamboo raft on the middle reaches of the Yangzi in Hubei Province. These huge rafts are disassembled and sold in markets at the lower reaches and used as construction scaffolding

posted in the streets outside. At No. 17 is a small conference room where Zhou Enlai met the press during negotiations. Upstairs is the secret radio equipment used for communicating directly with Mao Zedong in Yan'an.

The houses, now museums, still exude both the cloak-and-dagger flavour of the period, and the austerity and dedication of their erstwhile occupants.

■ FUZI MIAO (CONFUCIUS TEMPLE)

In the south of the city, near a stretch of the Qinhuai River, is a newly developed area where Qing-style buildings house shops and restaurants. The city fathers have recreated the bustling bazaar that clustered round the Song-dynasty Confucius Temple (Fuzi Miao) that stood here. The temple, destroyed by the Japanese in the 1940s, has been reconstructed. Fuzi Miao is in Gong-yuan Jie, off Jiankang Lu.

■ MING EXAMINATION HALL, GONGYUAN JIE

Imperial examinations were held at the capital every three years during the early Ming dynasty (1368–1644); even when the capital was moved to Beijing, candidates for high office travelled to Nanjing from nearby provinces. The Examination Hall comprised 20,600 tiny cubicles in which candidates were locked and kept guarded during the three-day examinations. Food was passed in daily to sustain the candidates through the trying ordeal.

A stone bridge and a square tower are all that remain of this huge establishment. Inside the tower are stelae inscribed with the rules of conduct for the examinations and the history of the hall itself.

■ SITE OF THE PALACE OF THE HEAVENLY KING (TIANWANGFU), CHANGJIANG LU

Xuyuan Garden, a lake, and a large marble boat are all that remain of the large palace built by Hong Xiuquan (1813–64), instigator of the Taiping Rebellion and self-styled 'Heavenly King' (see page 116). His palace was destroyed by the Qing troops after the defeat of the rebellion in 1864. Local Qing officials used the site as a yamen (offices). Later the Guomindang government buildings were erected on the site. These were the country's administrative headquarters between 1927 and 1937 (when the Japanese entered the city). The late Generalissimo Chiang Kai-shek's office was in this complex during that period. Today the Nanjing Municipal Party Committee occupies the buildings. Neither the garden nor the offices may be visited without a Public Security Bureau permit.

■ JIMINGSI (COCK CROW TEMPLE), BEIJIGE HILL

The halls date from the late Qing dynasty (1644–1911), but house Ming sculpture

(1368–1644). Since it was believed that the ghosts of those killed on this site—a Yuan-dynasty execution ground—needed appeasement, the first Ming emperor, Hongwu, decreed the construction of this temple. It was a nunnery until the Cultural Revolution (1966–76).

Sights Outside the City Centre

■ YUHUATAI (TERRACE OF THE RAIN OF FLOWERS)
A monument to 100,000 Communist revolutionaries killed on this site—used by the Guomindang as an execution ground—was erected in 1950. In the sixth century, the legend goes, a Buddhist monk, Yun Guang, lived and preached here. So eloquent was he that the heavens showered flowers upon him, and these turned into beautiful little agate stones. These rain-flower pebbles are sold to visitors in containers of water to enhance their coloration.

■ SIGHTS ON ZIJINSHAN (PURPLE AND GOLD MOUNTAIN)
The three peaks of Zijinshan (the highest is 448 metres, or 1,470 feet) form this evergreen scenic area east of Nanjing. Some of the city's most famous sights are to be seen in this region.

■ THE MING TOMB (MINGXIAO LING)
The first emperor of the Ming dynasty, Hongwu, was buried here in 1398, alongside his empress, Ma Hou, who died in 1382. The tomb, begun in 1381, is recorded as having taken convict labourers three years to complete. Most of the buildings of the mausoleum have been destroyed; the Taiping rebels plundered it in the 1800s. The tomb is in poor condition compared with those of Hongwu's descendants, who were buried outside Beijing after the capital was moved there. Remains of a cobbled path lead to the Spirit Way, the traditional guard of honour that lines the route to imperial tombs. Along the Spirit Way are pairs of stone animals alternately standing and lying, and, at the far end, effigies of warriors and civil servants. The bold and simple style of carving is typical of the early Ming period.

■ DR SUN YATSEN'S MAUSOLEUM
Nanjing's most famous landmark is the elegant blue and white mausoleum of Dr Sun Yatsen (1866–1925), father of the Chinese Republic. Dr Sun's body was kept at the Biyun Monastery in the Western Hills of Beijing until this mausoleum was completed in 1929. 'Universal Love' are the characters above the triple-arched gateway, through which an avenue of tall trees leads to the main gate, with 'The world belongs to everyone' in Chinese emblazoned on it. A flight of 392 marble steps leads to the memorial hall in which is a gypsum statue of a seated Dr Sun (sculpted in France by

a Polish friend, Landowski). Dr Sun's remains are beneath a recumbent marble statue of him (executed by Japanese associates) in the circular crypt behind the hall. The mausoleum was designed by Lu Yanzhi and the colours are those of the Guomindang flag.

■ ZIJINSHAN OBSERVATORY
Situated on one peak of Zijinshan, this third largest of China's observatories was built in 1934. There is a small but fascinating collection on display of magnificent Ming (1368–1644) reproductions of early astrological instruments: a celestial globe, an armillary sphere for detecting solar bodies, a gnomon (a sun and seasons dial) and an earthquake detector first made over 2,000 years ago. The last two instruments have had a disturbed history. In 1900, Germans absconded with the earthquake detector (which was then in the Beijing observatory) but it was returned, along with the other instruments taken as spoils of war, in 1919. In the early 1930s the Japanese tried unsuccessfully to remove the gnomon; they even cut the base in half.

If you climb onto the platform of one of the observatory domes you will find yourself above the tree line, and, unfurling below you, a marvellous view of Nanjing and the Yangzi.

■ LINGGU MONASTERY (VALLEY OF THE SOUL MONASTERY)
In order to build his grand mausoleum on an auspicious site, the Ming emperor Hongwu (reigned 1368–98) had first to remove an existing temple, the Linggusi, to its present wooded peak. All that remains of that Ming temple is the 46-metre (150 foot) long **Beamless Hall** (**Wuliang Dian**), made of brick with no supporting wooden beams. A handsome *pailou* or gateway leads to the hall. West of the hall is the flat **Coiled Dragons Stone**, found beside a nearby pool, on which monks once meditated. The present Linggu Monastery dates from the late Qing period and is occupied by a community of monks.

To the north of the Beamless Hall stands the nine-storeyed **Linggu Pagoda,** which was built by the Guomindang in 1929. For the energetic, the long climb to the top is rewarded with a fine view over wooded countryside.

SIGHTS ON QIXIA MOUNTAIN

For visitors spending more than a few days in Nanjing, a visit to these sites on Qixia Hill are strongly recommended. Seventeen kilometres (10.5 miles) east of Nanjing, the drive to the Buddhist grottoes and temple of Qixia takes the visitor through an area rich in tomb sites of the nobility of the Liang dynasty (502–57). In particular there are stone figures from the tombs of three of Emperor Wudi's brothers, Xiao Dan, Xiao Hui and Xiao Xiu. Xiao Dan's tomb includes a well-preserved stele on the back of a stone tortoise and two large stone winged lions. Xiao Xiu's tomb figures include wonderfully carved winged lions, tortoises and columns.

Mr Hu Zhenhao, one of the last of the Xiling Gorge trackers, famous for his performances of old boat songs, with his troupe based in Zigui, Hubei, original home of dragon boat races

■ QIXIA MONASTERY

First built in the fifth century, this monastery has repeatedly been destroyed and restored thereafter. The present temple buildings date from the early 20th century. Now serving as headquarters of the Jiangsu Branch of the Buddhist Association of China, the temple is an active centre of worship where the monks hold regular services. The monastery also boasts an exceptional library of 7,200 volumes of Buddhist scriptures. Behind the monastery is the **Sheli Pagoda**, one of the oldest stone pagodas south of the Yangzi River. This 15-metre (50-foot) high, five-storeyed pagoda was built in 601, and is embellished with detailed carvings of Buddha's life.

■ QIXIA THOUSAND BUDDHA CLIFF

There are more than 500 statues in nearly 300 niches and grottoes in the cliff-face near the monastery. The earliest date from the fifth century, and they continued to be carved until the Ming dynasty (1368–1644). Many of their heads were defaced or lopped off during the Cultural Revolution (1966–76). One figure is a 13-metre (43-foot) high Buddha, said to have been carved by Zhongzhang, son of the magistrate-turned-hermit, Ming Sengshao (who donated his home as the original Qixia Monastery).

Zhenjiang

Zhenjiang, on the south bank, with a population of 390,000, is situated in the middle of Jiangsu Province, at the junction of the Yangzi and the Grand Canal, 63 kilometres (40 miles) from Nanjing. It was the capital of the province during the Republican period (1911–49) when Nanjing was the national capital. Earlier Chinese travellers classified Zhenjiang's scenery as 'The Best Landscape under Heaven', and indeed the area known as the Southern Suburbs was often used as a theme in landscapes by famous Chinese painters. Marco Polo visited the city in the 13th century, commenting: 'The people of Zhenjiang live by industry and commerce; they produce much silk and brocade and the rustic flavour of the place is suitable for the production of many things.'

The American Nobel Prize-winning writer, Pearl Buck (1892–1973), author of *The Good Earth* and other novels about China, lived in Zhenjiang for 15 years before attending boarding school in Shanghai. Her missionary parents' house still stands in the northern part of the city, incorporated into a radio factory. Handicrafts include jade carvings, palace lanterns and screens of natural stone. Zhenjiang is also known for its black vinegar and pickled vegetables.

HISTORY OF ZHENJIANG

Zhenjiang, under various names, has existed for 2,500 years. In 213 BC, its importance as a ferry crossing led Emperor Qin Shihuangdi to conclude that Zhenjiang's *fengshui* (geomantic) powers were too strong. He ordered 3,000 prisoners to dig a tunnel through one of the hills to divert the influences.

During the convoluted politics of the Three Kingdoms period (220–65, *see* page 42), Sun Quan, ruler of the kingdom of Wu, made his capital here and Zhenjiang was the site of many 'mini-summits' on military strategy between the warring kingdoms. Thereafter the settlement grew steadily, benefitting greatly from the construction of the Grand Canal under the Sui dynasty (581–618). Its key location at the intersection of the Grand Canal and the Yangzi made it the hub of water transportation from the seventh century onwards.

Under the Song dynasty (960–1279) the city's development reached its height, producing fine silks, satins and silverware as tribute to the imperial court. Troops were stationed here to defend the river (*Zhenjiang* means 'guard the river')—a wise precaution, as it turned out, when they had to take on invading Jin troops in a naval battle near Jin Shan in 1130.

During the Opium War of 1842, Zhenjiang was bombarded by British men-of-war. Seven thousand British troops stormed the walled city, which was defended by only about 3,000 courageous Chinese soldiers. The governor of the city and his family committed suicide. On the British side, 105 soldiers were killed or wounded. This battle was a turning point, as it led to the signing of the Treaty of Nanking only a month later. The treaty provided for the surrender of Hong Kong to Britain and for the payment of 21 million Mexican dollars by the Chinese as indemnity.

The city was again captured in 1853 by the Taiping rebels (*see* page 116) and held by them for four years, which left it crippled for some time. A small foreign concession area was established in 1861. A H Rasmussen, a Scandinavian trader who lived in Zhenjiang for many years, wrote:

> Then I went into the silent street for a breath of fresh air and walked up and down the bund, three hundred paces one way and three hundred paces back. To get a little change I walked up and down the only cross street to the south gate of the Concession, two hundred paces one way and two hundred paces back.

Life was very restricted, and the hunting of wild boar in the surrounding hills became the main pastime for the resident foreigners.

Trade recovered, however. Customs house records show that in the first decade of the 20th century the value of goods transshipped in one year through Zhenjiang exceeded a staggering 35 million taels of silver (one tael is roughly 50 grammes or 1.8 ounces).

But the coming of the railway put an end to this spate of merchandise; by the 1920s, much of it was being conveyed by freight trains. Yet Zhenjiang is still a busy transportation hub. A new port at nearby Dagang has enhanced its importance and it is on the Shanghai–Nanjing railroad line. Industries include metallurgy, electronics and vehicle and ship construction.

What to See in Zhenjiang

With some 300 factories employing well over a third of its population of 390,000, Zhenjiang is now indisputably industrial. Yet it still enjoys the appellation 'City of Forests and Hills', which was coined by the celebrated landscape painter Mi Fu

Two hundred years ago Jinshan Temple stood on an island in the Yangzi River, now, due to silting, it has become part of the southern bank near Zhenjiang. The River can just be seen in the photograph running along the horizon

(1051–1107) because it is flanked on three sides by tree-clad mountains.

The busiest area of the city is within the confines of Zhengdong Lu, Jiefang Lu and Renmin Lu. The old city is further west, near Boxian Park. The foreign concession was there; its British consulate is now the **Zhenjiang Museum**. On Boxian Lu an old American church still retains the stone plaque set into a wall which reads, though not clearly:

First Baptist Church
Organized
... D 1885
Rebuilt 1921

■ XIAO MATOU JIE (SMALL JETTY STREET)

Take this charming little cobbled street through the oldest part of town. The rows of Qing-dynasty (1644–1911) buildings are intersected by stone arches at regular intervals. One of these is the **Zhaoguan Stupa**—5 metres (16 feet) high rising behind a stone archway—which dates from the Yuan dynasty (1279–1368). The names engraved on either side commemorate those who were officials of the prefecture when the *stupa* was restored in 1583.

The cobbled pathway was once lined with shops selling incense to devotees at Jin Shan Temple. West of the *stupa* is the **Western Ferry Crossing (Xi Jindu Jie)**. Its stone steps once led straight down to the riverside, where there was a ferry service to Jin Shan and the other side of the Yangzi. Marco Polo is said to have come ashore at this very spot.

■ JIN SHAN (GOLDEN HILL)

The 44-metre (144-foot) Golden Hill, with its famous monastery, was an island in the centre of the Yangzi until it merged with the river bank in the middle of the last century. Visitors used to take a ferry from the Western Ferry Crossing, and then rode mules to the top. Jin Shan Monastery was first built over 1,500 years ago. In its heyday, the monastery was looked after by 3,000 Buddhist monks.

Visitors may be shown the most interesting of the several sights and relics on Jin Shan. **Jin Shan Pagoda** was first built 1,400 years ago and rebuilt many times: in the Song dynasty as two pagodas, in the Ming as a single tower and three times in the Qing period. **Fa Hai** or **Pei Gong Cave** is identified by a statue of the monk Fa Hai, son of a Tang-dynasty prime minister. Fa Hai lived here when he came to the monastery, having first studied at Lushan. It is said that when the monk discovered a pot of gold, he gave it to the local officials. The emperor ordered that the gold be returned to Fai Hai, to rebuild the monastery, thereafter named Golden Hill Monastery.

The extraordinary folk tale of the White Snake is connected to Fa Hai. The story tells of a 1,000-year old white snake, Bai Suzhen, who, longing for a life among mortals, changed herself into a beautiful maiden. She married a young herbalist, Xu Xian, whom she first met on the famous Broken Bridge on the West Lake in Hangzhou. The happy couple set up business dispensing medicines, but Suzhen's magical cures aroused the anger of the powerful Buddhist monk, Fa Hai. His machinations put the couple through many trials and tribulations, including imprisonment of Xu Xian, before he was eventually defeated. At one point Xu Xian escaped through the **Bai Long Dong (White Dragon Cave)** on Jin Shan, for though narrow it is said to lead to Hangzhou, where the herbalist and Suzhen were reunited.

In the monastery, a bronze drum, presented in the Qing dynasty (1644–1911), is one of the treasures of the **Four Precious Rooms (Sibao Shi)**. It is believed to have belonged to Zhuge Liang (181–234, see page 42) and to have doubled as a cooking pot when not being beaten in war. Another is Su Dongpo's official mandarin belt of 20 jade pieces. Su apparently had to forfeit his belt when he lost a debate on Buddhism with his friend, the monk Fo Yin.

The scroll-adorned **Fo Dian (Buddha Hall)**, with its 18 *luohan* (disciples of Buddha) statues, is where the monks hold their services.

West of Jin Shan, along the road that runs beside an artificial lake, is **Zhongling Spring**, the 'Foremost Spring under Heaven'. It was graded by the Tang scholar, Lu Yu, whose *Book of Teas* listed and classified seven springs in China according to the water's compatibility with tea. Zhongling's water was judged the sweetest for brewing tea. The bubbling spring trickles into a small pool enclosed by bamboo groves, but today its water is anything but sweet.

■ BEIGU SHAN

Rising from the Yangzi the steep cliff face of the 53-metre (174-foot) high Beigu Shan was a natural fortification and was chosen by the King of Wu, Sun Quan, as the site of his capital, Tiewangcheng, in the third century. The Martyr's Monument now stands where the great Wu general, Zhou Yu, made his headquarters. The novel *Romance of the Three Kingdoms* (see page 42) contains many stories concerning Beigu Shan.

The exquisite **Iron Pagoda** dates from the Song dynasty (960–1279) and has an extraordinary history of survival. Erected in the 11th century on the site of an earlier pagoda, it had nine tiers. In the Ming dynasty (1368–1644), a tidal wave destroyed seven tiers, which were later replaced. In the Qing (1644–1911), the upper tiers were again destroyed, this time by lightning. Several Ming tiers were discovered nearby during restoration in 1961 and replaced in position above the only two remaining original Tang tiers. Over 2,000 Tang (618–907) relics were also found at that time. The **Ganlu (Sweet Dew) Temple** buildings now house painting exhibits.

The **Hen Stone** was carved into the shape of a ram at the end of the last century. It is believed that the King of Wu sat on this stone when planning his strategy for the great Red Cliff Battle (*see* page 93).

The pretty **Duojing Lou (Tower of Many Views)** is said to have been the dressing room of Liu Bei's wife, the sister of Sun Quan. Song-dynasty literati frequently held banquets in it.

Liu Bei's wife is said to have committed suicide from the **Jijiang Ting (Sacrificing to the River Pavilion)**. She threw herself into the river upon hearing of the death of her husband at Baidi Cheng (*see* pages 42 and 56), after his defeat by her brother, the treacherous Sun Quan.

The two **Shijian Shi (Sword Testing Stones)**, each split neatly in two, were reputedly cloven by the swords of Liu Bei and Sun Quan, who were at that time outwardly in alliance over regaining the city of Jiangling (present-day Jingzhou, *see* page 89) but each secretly plotting to betray the other.

The three characters *liu ma jian*—'Hold back the horse from the cliff—on the face below the hill, are associated with a story that also involves Liu and Sun. At a banquet together, Liu, who being from the northwest was an expert cavalryman but was less adept at naval warfare, said to Sun, 'Now I know why southerners can row boats so well, and northerners manage their horses.' Sun took offence at what he considered a backhanded compliment, and challenged Liu to a race. In a drunken state they leapt on to their horses. As they reached the cliff edge Liu reined in his horse, but Sun could not and was saved from death only at the last moment by Liu.

■ JIAO SHAN

Four kilometres (2.5 miles) northeast of Zhenjiang, the tiny island of Jiao Shan can be reached by a local ferry. It was named after a hermit scholar-monk, Jiao Guang of the Eastern Han period (25–220), who is said to have lived in what is known as the **Three Summons Cave**.

Thrice Jiao was invited by the emperor to take an official post, and thrice he refused. He lived to be 120 years old, treating and healing the local fisherfolk.

At the foot of the hill is **Dinghui Monastery (Monastery of Stability and Wisdom)**, built on the site of an earlier temple in the Tang dynasty (618–907). It was burnt down and rebuilt in the Ming (1368–1644). Old gingko trees stand in front of the main hall which contains some fine bronze *luohan* (disciples of Buddha) statues, presented by temples at Wutai Shan in Shanxi Province.

The chief attraction of the **Jiao Shan Forest of Tablets (Bei Lin)**, a collection of over 260 inscribed stones classified into literary, artistic and historic works, the earliest of which date from the Eastern Jin dynasty, is the White Crane Tablet cut with the calligraphy of Wang Yizhe (321–79). Wang was fond of white cranes (which symbolize longevity) and on seeing one on Jiao Shan asked if he could have it. The monk refused at first, but on learning Wang's identity agreed that he could collect the crane on his next visit.

Returning a year later, Wang discovered that the crane had died and had been buried, wrapped in yellow silk, on the hillside. His text of the sad story of the crane was preserved on a tablet on the hill. Later, during an earthquake, part of the inscription broke off and fell into the river. A thousand years later, in 1713, five pieces were recovered upstream, and were restored to their rightful place.

The **Cannon Platform** dates from the first Anglo-Chinese Opium War. (Another lies on Elephant Hill on the south bank of the Yangzi.) In the course of the war, British naval ships sailed up the river and, in a two-pronged attack, captured the stronghold, killing 500 Chinese troops. The walls—pockmarked with cannon shell—are made of rammed earth and sticky-rice water.

Near the top of the hill are viewing pavilions and the **Bie Feng Yan** cottage in which Zheng Banqiao (1693–1765), one of the Eight Eccentric Painters of the Yangzhou school, lived for five years.

■ ZHENJIANG MUSEUM

A fascinating survivor of the foreign concession in Zhenjiang is the former British Consulate at the foot of a knoll overlooking the port. The compound consists of seven buildings, a couple of which now form the city's museum. They house a collection of ancient bronzeware, celadon, porcelain, fabrics and a cache of Tang dynasty silverware (618–907) unearthed in the Danyang area in 1983. Outside, the anchor from the British frigate *HMS Amethyst*, and several canons brought back from Jiaoshan, recall Zhenjiang's involvement in the first Opium War.

Yangzhou

There is a little verse, much quoted in reference to Yangzhou, which goes something like this:

> Brilliant moonlight, orioles, flowers and pavilions of jade,
> All attest to the past and present glories of Yangzhou.

To these glories might also be added Yangzhou's tradition of producing beautiful women.

Yangzhou was one of the most important cities on the Grand Canal and is a delightful place to visit, retaining to some degree the feeling of its rich cultural and historical traditions. A vehicular ferry from Zhenjiang crosses the Yangzi and from the north bank the drive to Yangzhou takes half-an-hour. Many traditional arts and crafts are still practised: lacquerware, paper-cuts, lanterns, embroidery, *penjing* (miniature gardens) and seal carving.

Yangzhou has one of the great cuisines of China and every foreigner knows—indirectly—about it, for Yangzhou is the home of the worldwide favourite Chinese dish of fried rice (*Yangzhou chaofan*).

HISTORY OF YANGZHOU

The city's history began over 2,400 years ago in the Spring and Autumn period (770–476 BC); one of the early nine provincial areas of China was called after it. The Sui emperor, Yangdi, initiated the construction of the Grand Canal here in 605, which eventually made Yangzhou the hub of land and water transportation. Emperor Yangdi visited the city three times in grand dragon-boats. He built a palace, retired and was buried here, after being assassinated in 618. Yangzhou was also a centre of classical learning and religion. Emperors, prime ministers and men of letters through the ages visited Yangzhou and many held official positions, including the great traveller Marco Polo, who was governor general of the city for three years.

By the Tang dynasty (618–907) Yangzhou's trading links with Arab merchants were well established. A foreign community numbering about a thousand lived in the city. It was said that 'at night a thousand lanterns lit up the clouds'. The economy was based on the salt monopoly and on grain shipments to the capital.

Yangzhou, along with so many other middle and lower Yangzi cities, suffered badly during the Taiping Rebellion in the mid-19th century (*see* page 116). In addition, the silting of the Yangzi and the flooding of the Grand Canal gradually undermined its entrepôt role, as grain shipments were increasingly transported by sea via Shanghai, rather than along the Grand Canal. Changes in the salt administration and the arrival of the railways were the *coup de grâce* in Yangzhou's decline.

During the late 18th century an individualistic school of painters sprang up, known as the Eight Eccentrics of Yangzhou, whose bold style has a strong following today.

WHAT TO SEE IN YANGZHOU

The streets of Yangzhou reveal much that is charming and interesting. Stroll down Guoqing Lu past craftsmen painting mirrors and making bamboo steamers and cloth shoes, then along Dujiang Lu where wooden-fronted shops, partitioned with rattan matting, sell household goods, basketware and fireworks, and itinerant sugarcane vendors hawk their wares. The road eventually reaches the Grand Canal, where, from the bridge, boat life can be observed as it passes by. The courtyards of the small, grey-tiled houses are cluttered with pots of flowers and miniature *penjing* plants—a speciality of the region. Rows of white cabbage and strips of turnip hang out to dry. One may also walk along the small canals.

The Imperial Jetty, where the Qing emperors disembarked, is situated on the canal in front of Xiyuan Hotel. Visit also **Yechun Yuan** where a poetry club used to meet in the Qing dynasty (1644–1911). It is now a tea-house and specializes in Yellow Bridge Buns, which were first created to supply the troops during the Sino-Japanese War. Further on is the **Luyang Cun**, a garden filled with miniature plants, goldfish and birds.

■ SLENDER WEST LAKE (SHOUXI HU)

This is a beautiful man-made lake dating from the Tang dynasty (618–907) and

THE GRAND CANAL —Judy Bonavia

The Grand Canal zigzags some 2,500 kilometres (1,554 miles) down the length of eastern China and remains the longest man-made waterway in the world. In ancient times it was crucial in the transportation of grain from the fertile Yangzi delta to the relatively barren north, and in developing communications across the vast territory that the waterway system served. From the Yellow River valley, from which Chinese civilization sprang, culture and learning spread southwards along the canal, until by the Tang dynasty (618–907) such cities as Yangzhou and Hangzhou had themselves become centres of art and philosophy.

The first link in this canal system was constructed in the fifth century BC by the King of Wu to facilitate his invasion of the Kingdom of Ji to the north. Other canals were constructed as political and economic demands arose. It was the Sui emperor Yangdi who, in the seventh century, set about creating an inter-communicating system linking his capital of Luoyang with the rice lands of the Yangzi River plains. The network was extended to the northern city, later called Beijing, to supply his armies, then fighting the Koreans. Tens of thousands of men and women were conscripted to labour on these projects, and to plant trees along the banks.

Ma Shumou, the emperor's cruel overseer, was known as Mahu—'Ma the Barbarous'. Yangzhou mothers to this day chastise their children by threatening 'Mahu will get you'. It was reputed that during the building of the Grand Canal he demanded a daily meal of steamed two-year old child.

During the Tang dynasty (618–907) over 300,000 tons of grain were shipped northwards annually under the escort of 120,000 soldiers.

When the Mongol Yuan dynasty (1279–1368) established its capital in present-day Beijing, the need for a rapid supply of grain, unimpeded by pirates along the sea route, led to the digging of a direct canal northwards, which shortened the route by some 700 to 800 kilometres (435 to 500 miles). The reduced length of 1,782 kilometres (1,108 miles) was bordered by a paved highway allowing travellers to cover the distance in 40 days.

Throughout its history the canal supplied not only the essentials of life but also the luxuries. Scholars and officials travelled on it to and from the capital for imperial examinations or affairs of state. Emperor Yangdi's retinue, in magnificent boats styled as dragons, tigers and birds, was pulled by 80,000 trackers along it.

During the Qing dynasty (1644–1911) official corruption, flooding and silting caused the gradual decline of the Grand Canal. Twelve thousand bridges span the canal, which in recent years has been dredged and repaired. Water from the Yangzi is being diverted along this age-old channel for irrigation of the northern plains and the cities of Beijing and Tianjin. Stretches of it are now open to tourism.

surrounded by weeping willows and pavilions. The Fishing Platform at the end of the Dyke of Spring Willows was reputedly used by Emperor Qianlong (reigned 1736–96). Through its arches different views of the beautiful **Five Pavilion Bridge (Wuting Qiao)**, built in 1757, are presented. The red pillars of the pavilions with their yellow-tiled roofs rest on 15 stone arches; extravagant claims are made about the splendid moonlit scene at the bridge at the Mid-autumn Festival—in a particularly auspicious year the moon is said to be reflected in the water under each arch. Near the bridge is a white *stupa*, whose origin is attributed to Emperor Qianlong. It seems that he remarked on a visit that though this scenic spot reminded him of Beihai Park in Beijing, it was a pity that there was no white *stupa* to complete the resemblance. The zealous local officials worked through the night to carve a full-sized *stupa* from salt. The emperor was duly impressed and, when he returned north, the permanent version that stands today was built. **The Friendship Hall** contains a stone tablet with a description of Marco Polo's three-year governorship in Yangzhou, and his portrait. The lovely Yu Garden was built in 1915 as the residence of the local warlord, Yu Baoshan.

■ WENFENG PAGODA
This seven-tiered wooden and brick pagoda stands beside a busy stretch of the Grand Canal south of the city, where boats load and unload goods—bamboo matting, soya beans, rice and cotton. Most of the boats are made of concrete; very few are of wood. Men beating gongs parade up and down with carts; they do the shopping for the boat-people who are too busy to go ashore and do their own. The Pagoda offers a good overview of the town.

■ XIANHE MOSQUE (FAIRY CRANE MOSQUE)
This is one of the four famous old mosques of China (the others are in Guangzhou, Hangzhou and Quanzhou). It was first built in 1275 to serve the needs of the Arab traders and was rebuilt twice in the Ming dynasty (1368–1644). Its ancient pine and gingko trees are believed to be around 800 years old. The mosque is supposed to resemble a crane in shape: the main entrance is the head; the wells on either side, the eyes; the left-hand path, the neck; the prayer hall, the body; the north and south halls, the wings.

Arabic scrolls executed in Chinese calligraphic style hang in one of the halls. There are some 3,600 Hui (Muslims) in Yangzhou, but the congregation at Friday prayers is less than 50. To see this mosque on Wenhe Lu, first check with your guide or CITS whether permission has to be obtained in advance. Normally neither the mosque nor Puhaddin's tomb (see below) is open to the general public, but wangle a visit if you can.

■ TOMB OF PUHADDIN

Puhaddin was a 16th-generation descendant of the Prophet Mohammed, founder of Islam. He came to China in the second half of the 13th century and was in Yangzhou between 1265 and 1275, helping to build the Fairy Crane Mosque. He travelled to Shandong Province to spread the word of Islam, but became ill and died there. He was buried, according to his wish, in Yangzhou.

A fine, carved white marble stairway leads to the cemetery. The majority of the 25 tombs here are those of Chinese Muslims but a few are the tombs of early Arab traders; the architectural style of the tombs is completely Arabian.

■ YANGZHOU MUSEUM

This building was originally erected in 1772 around the tomb of Shi Kefa (1601–45) who was in command of Yangzhou when the Qing armies moved south to consolidate their power. A supporter of the Ming dynasty, Shi and his 4,000 troops held out against the Qing army for ten days, five times refusing to surrender and fighting to the death. The museum's most prized possession is its collection of 18th-century paintings and calligraphy by the Eight Eccentrics of Yangzhou, whose rejection of the orthodox style of the day was a major breakthrough in Chinese painting.

■ GARDENS

The rich salt merchants of Yangzhou left a legacy of many exquisite gardens. The delightful **Ge Garden** north of Dongguan Jie was the home of a rich 19th-century salt merchant, Huang Yingtai. Its architecture, bamboo groves and landscaping are typical of the famous private gardens of Suzhou. The garden got its name from its bamboo leaves, shaped like the Chinese character *ge*. On Xuningmen Jie is the popular **He Garden**, built by He Zhidao. It once belonged to the Qing Court's ambassador to France, and some Western architectural influences can be seen.

■ WENCHANG GE (PAVILION OF FLOURISHING CULTURE)

This 'mini' Temple of Heaven, dedicated to the god of literary success, is three storeys high and took ten years to build; just before completion it burnt down, only to be immediately rebuilt in 1585. Originally situated on a bridge across a canal, the area was transformed into a wide roadway, so Wenchang Ge now stands at the intersection of Wenhe Jie and Shita Jie. Nearby is the **Stone Pagoda** (Shi Ta), a highly valued Tang-dynasty relic. Its six sides are decorated with floral patterns.

■ TIANNING TEMPLE (TEMPLE OF HEAVENLY TRANQUILLITY)

The present buildings date from the Ming dynasty (1368–1644), though a temple existed here in the Song dynasty (960–1279). The Qing emperor, Qianlong, had a travel lodge built on one of his inspection tours. The temple is next to the Xiyuan Hotel.

■ DAMING TEMPLE

Daming Temple is part of a complex of buildings. The temple was built in the fifth century. Large incense burners with bells stand in front of the main hall in which services are held daily at 4 pm.

The temple has strong ties with Japan. The Buddhist abbot, Jian Zhen (688– 763), was invited to teach in Japan, and made five attempts to go there, but failed each time. It was on his sixth attempt, at the age of 66 and by then blind, that he succeeded in reaching the Japanese capital of Nara where he set up a study centre at one of the temples. His contribution in bringing understanding of Chinese literature and arts, architecture, medicine and printing to Japan was commemorated in 1963, when a number of Chinese and Japanese Buddhists decided to build the **Jian Zhen Memorial Hall**. The walls are decorated with murals depicting his journeys. In 1980 the Japanese donated a wooden statue of Jian Zhen, a copy of the beautiful lacquer statue of the monk in the Nara Temple in Japan. In front of the wooden statue is an incense burner presented by Emperor Hirohito of Japan.

Pingshan Hall was built by the great Song-dynasty scholar, statesman and poet, Ouyang Xiu, in 1048 to entertain his guests when he was prefect of Yangzhou. A statue of him now stands in the hall. A student of his, Su Dongpo, also an official in Yangzhou, wrote a commemorative poem about Ouyang, which is engraved in stone on the walls.

In the gardens of the temple is another of the seven great springs of China, mentioned in the Tang-dynasty *Book of Teas*. This one is known as the 'Fifth Spring under Heaven' (*see* page 115).

Parts of the Tang (618–907) city-walls can be seen in the vicinity of Daming Temple and on **Guanyin Hill**, the site of the Sui emperor Yangdi's palace.

Nantong

Nantong is one of the 14 port cities opened to foreign investment projects under China's current policies of modernization. The city is an integral part of the Shanghai Economic Zone. The population of 7.4 million is engaged in industrial production, especially textiles. It is hoped that textile, precision machinery and communications industries will be established either as joint ventures or entirely foreign enterprises. Ten thousand-ton vessels berth at its deep-water harbour.

One of the city's heroes was Cao Gong, who in 1557 successfully defended the town against Japanese pirates roaming the coast of China. His heroic exploits earned him a high official position which he refused to accept. Cao was killed in another pirate raid shortly after. The **Cao Gong Zhu Memorial Temple** was built in his honour.

Sailing the Yangzi

I sailed 1,500 miles downstream, from Chungking to Shanghai. Every mile of it was different; but there were 1,200 miles I did not see. It crosses ten provinces, 700 rivers are joined to it—all Yangtze statistics are hopeless, huge and ungraspable; they obscure rather than clarify. And since words have a greater precision than numbers, one day I asked a Chinese ship captain if he thought the river had a distinct personality.

He said, 'The mood of the river changes according to the season. It changes every day. It is not easy. Navigating the river is always a struggle against nature. And there is only one way to pilot a ship well.' He explained—he was smiling and blowing smoke out of his nostrils— 'It is necessary to see the river as an enemy.'

Later a man told me that in the course of one afternoon he had counted nine human corpses bobbing hideously down the river.

The Yangtze is China's main artery, its major waterway, the source of many of its myths, the scene of much of its history. On its banks are some of its greatest cities. It is the fountainhead of superstition; it provides income and food to half the population. It is one of the most dangerous rivers in the world, in some places one of the dirtiest, in others one of the most spectacular. The Chinese drink it and bathe in it and wash clothes in it and shit in it. It represents both life and death. It is a wellspring, a sewer and a tomb; depthless in the gorges, puddle-shallow at its rapids. The Chinese say if you haven't been up the Great River, you haven't been anywhere.

They also say that in the winter, on the river, the days are so dark that when the sun comes out the dogs bark at it. Chungking was dark at nine in the morning, when I took the rattling tin tram on the cog railway that leads down the black crags which are Chungking's ramparts, down the sooty cliffs, past the tenements and billboards ('Flying Pigeon Bicycles', 'Seagull Watches', 'Parrot Accordions') to the landing stage. A thick sulpherous fog lay over the city, a Coketown of six million . . . Doctor Ringrose, who was from Leeds, sniffed and said, 'That is the smell of my childhood.'

Paul Theroux, Sailing Through China, *1984*

East of the city is **Lang Shan** (**Wolf Hill**), said to be haunted by the spirit of a white wolf. The temple on top is dedicated to a Song-dynasty Buddhist monk, whom legend endowed with magical powers over water demons. Boat people prayed to him for safe journeys. The main hall contains models of different types of river craft. At the base of Lang Shan is the **Five Hills Park**.

■ BAOSHAN

The giant Baoshan Steel Works on the south bank, near the mouth of the Huangpu River, is planned to be the largest in China. Japanese and West German technology and plant are being used. In the early stages the project ran into difficulties, not the least of which was the choice of site—marshy ground that caused subsidence. More-over, the estuary was found to be too shallow to allow 100,000-ton freighters bearing imported iron ore to unload. The first phase of the mill began operation in 1985.

■ HUANGPU RIVER

Just below Baoshan, boats pass by a large lighthouse and between buoys to turn south into the Huangpu River, on the last stage of the journey from Chongqing to Shanghai. The 72-kilometre (44.7-mile) cruise today takes one through the heart of Shanghai's port; on either side of the muddy river stretch wharf installations with facilities to handle ocean-going ships of 25,000 tons, and an annual shipping volume of about 100 million tons. This is China's largest port and its busiest. Apart from the hundreds of foreign and Chinese registered ships, the river is busy all day long with ferries, naval and police craft, lighters and dredges.

The Huangpu is 114 kilometres (70 miles) in length, rising from Dianshan Lake southwest of Shanghai. Its banks were once simply mud flats. The river is subject to heavy silting from the Yangzi and requires constant dredging to keep the channels free.

Soon after entering the river, on the western bank is the area known as **Wusong**, where in 1842, during the Opium War, a fleet of British warships and support vessels opened fire on the ill-defended Chinese fort and its miles of earthworks. After a two-hour bombardment they forced their way up to Suzhou Creek and on to Shanghai. The fort was heroically defended but the Chinese were no match for the British fleet. Among the many Chinese casualties was a highly respected 76-year-old admiral who had been at sea for 50 years and who, it was said, wrapped himself in cotton wool before his battles to make himself invulnerable. This was a decisive battle, for it enabled the fleet to occupy Shanghai and move on up the Yangzi; later in the year, the Treaty of Nanking was signed, opening many Chinese cities to foreign trade.

Before the opium trade was legitimized in 1860, opium clippers and steamers unloaded their cargo on to hulks permanently moored at Wusong, Shanghai's outer anchorage, before they were smuggled into the hinterland.

Gradually Shanghai's imposing skyline appears as boats sidle up to the berth alongside Zhongshan Lu, once known as the Bund, and lined with impressive European-style buildings from a bygone era.

Twin-hulled tourist boats take visitors on a four-hour river trip through Shanghai's docks and up the Huangpu River to the Yangzi. The boats leave from the wharf opposite the Peace Hotel.

Shanghai

A conurbation of over 13 million people, Shanghai is China's second-largest city and is one of the four centrally administered cities in the country, the other three being Beijing, Tianjin and Chongqing. It is also one of China's most important industrial and cultural centres.

To most foreigners, Shanghai conjures up stories of adventure and intrigue, of vice and pleasure. Many of these were probably no exaggeration, for it was a dynamic, violent and colourful city. Most of the European-style quarters of the old International Settlement and the French Concession areas can still be seen, though they are much in need of repair. One can still clearly imagine the extraordinary life of pre-1949 Shanghai.

History of Shanghai

The name Shanghai, which means 'on the sea', was first used in AD 960 when the settlement was a backward fishing village. In 1554, the town was surrounded by a 7-metre (23-foot) high crenellated city wall and a moat to protect it against the frequent incursions of Japanese pirates. By the 17th century there were signs of growing wealth, but when the British troops stormed its undefended walls in 1842, Shanghai was still only a county town of little importance.

The first foreign settlement was established in 1843, when the newly-appointed British Consul arrived to negotiate for a 138-acre (just over 0.5 square kilometres) site north of the existing city. This site was joined with the American Settlement, founded in 1848 north of Suzhou Creek, to form the International Settlement in 1863. Subsequent negotiations with the Chinese increased the area of the International Settlement to more than 5,500 acres (about 22 square kilometres). The French Concession was established on 164 acres (about 0.6 square kilometres) in 1849 and was finally extended to about 2,500 acres (about 10 square kilometres). The Japanese, also, had secured a concession by the end of the last century, which became a centre for cotton-spinning factories. These settlements were self-administered and were outside Chinese government jurisdiction.

The old Chinese City, occupied by one group of the Taiping rebels—the

Dagger Society—between 1853 and 1855, became the scene of lawlessness and fighting. The foreign community, concerned for its own safety, formed the Shanghai Volunteer Corps, recruited from local traders and diplomats. They were even prepared to take on the imperial troops: backed by British and American officers and men from visiting warships, the volunteers issued an ultimatum for the troops' removal, an action which precipitated the Battle of Muddy Flat in 1854. The imperial troops were duly driven away from their encampment, which was the site of the old racecourse, now the People's Park.

Shanghai was again threatened by the Taiping rebels in the 1860s, but they were quelled by the Ever Victorious Army made up of foreigners and Chinese, established for this very purpose. An American, Frederick Townsend Ward, a Frenchman, Henri A. Burgevine, and a Briton, Charles George Gordon ('Chinese Gordon', later of Khartoum fame), took successive command and were all made officers of the Qing Imperial Army (*see* page 116).

The nationwide upheavals in the 20th century—the Boxer Rebellion, the 1911 Revolution, the Sino-Japanese War—took their toll on Shanghai's millions. Hundreds of thousands of Chinese poured into the foreign settlements for protection and then stayed on. Nevertheless, Shanghai continued to flourish as an entrepôt with its staple exports of tea and silk, and imports of piece goods and opium. Banking played an important part in this great trading city, which had its own stock exchange.

The foreigners' lifestyle was grand and lavish for those who could afford to participate in clubs, race meetings, paper chases and nightclubs. The arrival in the 1930s of some 25,000 White Russian refugees enlivened the nightlife of cabarets and dance halls in 'Frenchtown', as the French Concession was called by the Anglo-Saxons. Chinese secret societies controlled the seamy side of Shanghai life, and the city was the Hollywood of China with a thriving movie industry.

But the Shanghai workers were subjected to appalling working conditions, overcrowding and exploitation, a situation leading inevitably to industrial unrest and revolutionary activity. The Communist Party of China was founded in Shanghai in 1921 at a secret meeting in the French Concession. The Party fomented strikes and uprisings—some of them actually planned by the late Premier Zhou Enlai—but these activities were violently suppressed by the Nationalist government. This was a period of debate among Chinese intellectuals, who were influenced by the philosophies and experience of the more industrialized West. Many of these Chinese had studied abroad or at missionary institutions of higher learning in Shanghai.

The beginning of the Sino-Japanese War saw bombing and fierce fighting in and around Shanghai, but the foreign concessions were not occupied by the Japanese until after the bombing of Pearl Harbour, when Allied nationals were interned.

In 1945, at the end of the war, the Guomindang government declared an end to all extra-territoriality, so Shanghai reverted to Chinese control.

When a People's Republic was proclaimed in China at the end of the civil war, foreigners and Chinese industrialists, fleeing communism, left Shanghai, many re-establishing themselves in Hong Kong.

Because of its long history of foreign capitalist exploitation and 'bourgeois attitudes', adherents of the Cultural Revolution in the 1960s and '70s were particularly vociferous in Shanghai, which became the headquarters of the so-called Gang of Four, the ultra-leftist elements of this chaotic period.

When China began to reform her economic system and opened her doors to the outside world, one imagined that there would be a resurgence of the entrepreneurial spirit in Shanghai. But this did not happen. Until recently, Shanghai has been starved of investment, Beijing having siphoned off much of its huge earnings. The city could hardly make the best of the winds of change since it had been left with roads, housing and factories dating back to the 1930s and '40s. As the population continued to grow, the problems of housing and traffic congestion grew ever more acute.

However, in 1988, Beijing and Shanghai entered a new revenue agreement. Instead of surrendering more than three-quarters of its annual revenues, Shanghai began contributing a fixed amount to the central government and keeping any surpluses for its own use. The development plans to revitalize Shanghai could scarcely be more ambitious: bridges; tunnels; an urban subway system; suburban housing; the technical upgrading and expansion of its textile industry; the building of a microelectronics industry in Caohejing, a would-be Silicon Valley; and the establishment of a new port and free trade and export processing zone in Pudong.

WHAT TO SEE IN SHANGHAI

While Shanghai's historical monuments may not compare with China's older cities, the city's appeal lies in its vitality, its rather run-down 1930s European architecture in a medley of styles, and its bustling, tree-lined streets, crammed with shops. Above all, Shanghai still has a style and flair quite different from any other Chinese city.

■ THE BUND (WAITAN)

Walking along Zhongshan Lu, you can enjoy the faded grandeur of old Shanghai, for this was the Bund, where the great trading houses and banks had their headquarters. On one side is a line of imposing 1930s European buildings, while on the other is the Huangpu River. The Bund has undergone a face-lift recently, which included raising the level of the breakwater to prevent flooding. The raised pedestrian promenade gives a good view of the Huangpu River with the futuristic-looking buildings of the new Pudong area rising on the other side.

Dongfeng Hotel was the old Shanghai Club, whose Long Bar was, in its heyday, the longest in the world. The Municipal People's Government of Shanghai offices are in the columned building that was the Hongkong and Shanghai Bank headquarters, built in 1921; the green-roofed **Peace Hotel** was the handsome Cathay Hotel, where Noel Coward wrote his play *Private Lives* in 1928. The Palace Hotel, opposite, now part of the Peace Hotel, was Sassoon House (named after one of Shanghai's Jewish tycoons). The **Bank of China** is in one of the few buildings still run by its original occupants. As before, the improved riverside promenade of the Bund continually throngs with Shanghai residents, who stroll about in the hot summer evenings and in the mornings practise *taijiquan* and martial arts.

At the end of the Bund, where Suzhou Creek meets the Huangpu, is **Huangpu Park**. It was first laid out by the British, who called it the Public Gardens. In the old days British residents held Sunday afternoon concerts and promenaded there. Though the regulations of the International Settlement did indeed forbid Chinese (other than servants and nannies) as well as dogs from the Gardens, the infamous sign 'No Dogs or Chinese Allowed' never existed. The waterfront building with the clock tower is the old Customs House.

■ SOME POPULAR SHOPPING STREETS

Nanjing Lu, the main shopping street of Shanghai, is divided into two sections, East and West, and stretches for nearly 10 kilometres (6 miles) from the Bund to Jiangsu Lu. For the Chinese, Shanghai offers the best shopping in the country, so this street is constantly jammed with out-of-towners as well as local shoppers. Nanjing Lu passes People's Park and the Municipal Library, the site of the former racecourse. English-speaking Shanghainese gather here, especially on Sunday mornings, to practise among themselves.

Another important shopping street is **Huaihai Lu**, which was the main street of the French Concession, then called Avenue Joffre.

Book stores—antiquarian and modern—are a speciality of **Fuzhou Lu**, as well as stationery and calligraphy accoutrements, though in earlier times it was a red-light district.

■ THE OLD TOWN AND HUXINTING TEA-HOUSE

Renmin Lu and Zhonghua Lu form the perimeters of the old city wall (destroyed in 1912) that enclosed the Chinese City. Still within this area, which includes the famous Yu Garden, visitors jostle in the ever-crowded alleys of the bazaar, whose small shops, restaurants and tea-houses provide local specialities of all description. The narrow streets nearby reveal an intimate and fascinating picture of daily life. Near the old town is Fuyu Lu—the flea market for antiques where people bring in the odd old items for sale by bargaining—before they get to the official shops.

Should you get tired of walking around the Old Town you can always rest in the beautiful old Huxinting (mid-lake) Tea-house. This five-sided pavilion stands in the middle of a rectangular pool near the entrance to the Yu Garden, connected to land by the Bridge of Nine Turnings (zigzagged, it is said, because evil spirits cannot go round corners).

■ YU GARDEN (YUYUAN)
This Garden of Leisurely Repose on the northeast side of the old Chinese Town was first established in 1559 by a mandarin named Pan. Laid out by a landscape artist, Zhang Nanyang, it has become one of the most renowned gardens in southern China. As the Pan family fortunes declined, the garden was neglected and overgrown until it was restored in 1760 by the local gentry. It became the headquarters of the Dagger Society in 1853, during the early part of the Taiping Rebellion, and was badly damaged. Part of the garden became the bazaar and local guildhalls, but over 20,000 square metres (24,000 square yards) remain of tall rockeries, halls, ponds and pavilions linked by zigzag corridors. The **Spring Hall**, used by the Dagger Society, houses exhibits of coins and weapons from that period. The five-ton porous **Exquisite Jade Rock** is one of the attractions: legend claims that when it was discovered some 900 years ago, it joined Emperor Huizong's collection of weird and grotesque rocks before finding a resting place in Yu Garden.

■ JADE BUDDHA TEMPLE (YUFO SI), ANYUAN LU
The yellow-walled monastery was established on this site in 1928. Its two jade Buddhas (out of five brought back from Burma in 1882 by the priest Hui Gen) were first kept in a suburb of Shanghai. Three halls make up the monastery complex. In the Jade Buddha Hall is the tranquil 2-metre (6.5-foot) high seated statue of Sakyamuni, while downstairs in the Reclining Buddha Hall is the white jade image of Sakyamuni in repose. Precious statues of the Northern Wei (386–534) and Tang (618–907) dynasties are on display in the monastery's exhibition hall, along with hand-copied Tang-dynasty Buddhist scriptures and paintings. Over 70 monks hold daily services. The monastery runs a vegetarian restaurant whose menu boasts 'meat' dishes such as pickled duck, sliced eel and chicken, all made of beancurd and vegetables. Crackling rice and mushroom soup is recommended.

■ SHANGHAI MUSEUM OF ART AND HISTORY
The newly opened museum is without doubt the finest in all of China and must rank among the great museums of the world. This is a new modern display, with sound and even a holographic movie kiosk. The artefacts of Shanghai's commercial past are revealing and nostalgic. While the city rapidly tears down more of its heritage, this museum is a great look back. 1288 Hongqiao Road. Tel. 2755-5595. Open daily (9am–4pm); Sundays, holidays closes at 3.30pm.

■ LONGHUA PAGODA AND TEMPLE

Situated in Shanghai's southwest area, the pagoda and temple were originally built between the 10th and the 13th centuries—historical records vary as to the exact dates. The present seven-storeyed pagoda is just over 40 metres (130 feet) high and dates from the early Song dynasty, but was restored at the end of the Qing (1644–1911). The Longhua Temple nearby is a complex of five halls flanked by bell and drum towers; the sound of the evening bell of Longhua was known as one of the old traditions of Shanghai. A flower terrace, overlooked from a tea-room, is also one of the attractions of the temple, for in its peony gardens there is a 100-year-old peony said to have been planted first in a Hangzhou temple during the reign of Emperor Xianfeng and later transplanted here. Engravings on a boundary stone indicate that the stone was placed at the southwest corner of this temple during the Five Dynasties period (907–960). West of the temple is **Longhua Park**, once part of the temple's peach orchard, and now replanted and expanded.

■ SHANGHAI BOTANICAL GARDENS

South of the Longhua Pagoda, the gardens' greenhouses, bamboo groves and flower gardens cover some 67 hectares (165 acres) of land. Among the gardens' miniature *penjing* trees is a pomegranate over 240 years old.

■ REVOLUTIONARY SITES

Several buildings reflect the city's revolutionary history. In a two-storeyed building at 76 Xingye Lu, the Communist Party of China was founded in 1921; it is proudly shown to visitors as the site of the First National Congress of the Communist Party of China. The former residence (1946) of the late premier Zhou Enlai is situated at 73 Sinan Lu, while at 7 Xiangshan Lu, the founder of modern China, Dr Sun Yatsen, and his wife Madame Soong Chingling lived between 1918 and 1924. Madame Soong, who lived much of her life in Shanghai, was made honorary chairman of the People's Republic of China upon her death in 1981. Her residence at 1843 Huaihai Lu, furnished as it was in her lifetime, is open to the public.

China's great revolutionary writer Lu Xun (1881–1936) lived in a three-storeyed house at 9 Dalu New Village, Shanyin Lu, from 1933 until his death. He is buried in Hongkou Park and nearby, in the Park, is a museum dedicated to his life and work.

■ SHANGHAI ZOO, HONGQIAO LU, NEAR THE AIRPORT

The zoo houses over 350 species of animals including giant pandas from Sichuan, golden-haired monkeys—which once frequented the Yangzi gorges—and rare Yangzi River alligators.

Shanghai

N ↑

0   0.5   1 km
0   0.3   0.6 miles

to Nanjing, Beijing
Jiaotong Lu
Zhenbei Lu
Caoyang Lu
Zhongshan Bei L
Cao'an Lu
Wuning
Lu
Chang

Beixingjing Nursery Garden

Jinsha Hotel ★

Changfeng Park

Wutong

River

(Suzhou Creek)

Zhongshan Park

Beichai Lu

Jiangsu

Wanhangdu Lu

Changning Lu

Zhongshan Xi Lu

Equatoria Hotel

Tianshan Park

Jing'an Guesthouse ★
Sh

Yan'an Xi Lu

Huashan Lu

Westin Tai Ping Yang Hotel ★

Holiday Inn Crowne Plaza Shanghai ★

Ch

Yangtze New World ★ Hotel

Galaxy Hotel ★

HONGQIAO AIRPORT ✈

Shanghai Zoo

Rainbow ★ Hotel

Former Residence of Soong Ching-ling

Lu

Huaihai Xi Lu

Huashan Lu

Hongqiao

Airport Hotel ★

Hotel Nikko ★ Longbai

Cypress Hotel

New Garden Hotel ★

Cherry Holiday ★ Villa

Soong ● Ching-ling's Tomb

Hengshan ★ Hotel

Hengshan Lu

Xujiahui ● Cathedral

Xujiahui ●

Tian Ma Hotel ★

Wuzhong Lu

Hongmei Lu

Sheraton Hua Ting Hotel ★

Jianguo ★ Hotel

Xietu

● Shanghai Stadium
Shanghai Stadium

Olympic ★ Hotel

Zhongsha

★	Hotel
▬▬▬	Ring Road
▬▬▬	Railway
●───	Shanghai Metro
●─╌─	Shanghai Metro # 2 Line Proposed Route
Xujiahui	Metro Station

Completed in early 1995, the new ring road expressway, raised above the existing Zhongshan Lu, reduces the journey time from the airport to the city centre to around 40 minutes in normal trffic conditions.

Cemetery of Martyrs

Longhua Park

Longhua Pagoda

Caoxi Nan Lu

to Hangzhou

Caobao Lu

The Flowers on the Sea

A 19th-century novel by Han Bangqing, The Singsong Girls of Shanghai, begins with a prologue in which the author dreams he is walking on a sea bobbing with flowers. The meaning of this will not be lost on the average Chinese reader, for Shanghai means Above-the-Sea and 'flower' is a euphemism for prostitute.

Prostitution was one of Shanghai's established institutions. The singsong houses (some of which remain standing in Shantou Lu and Fuzhou Lu, though long turned to other uses) had names like the House of Sure Satisfaction and the Hall of Beauties inscribed in red on the glass lanterns outside their doors. The high-class ones would have a strip of red paper posted on the door with the courtesan's name on it. Stepping inside, the patron found himself in a parlour with little rooms partitioned off it. The sound of music might reach his ears—for the girls were entertainers as well as prostitutes—as servant girls appeared to welcome him with tea and bowls of nuts and sweetmeats. A meal would be laid out, with waiters scurrying to bring the caller bowls of cooked dishes and cups of warmed wine.

Next, a pipe would be offered. Lying on a lacquered divan, the patron would watch as his favourite courtesan heated his opium, rolling the paste into a pellet and roasting it over a flame.

With its maidservants, 'aunties' (madams), drinking parties and regular customers, the Shanghai singsong houses had a domestic feel to them. To call them whorehouses would be to do them a disservice. Some of them were select establishments, frequented only by the well-heeled. The most select were the shuyu, or 'storytellers' residences', so named because many singsong girls had begun their careers as teahouse balladeers.

The higher the grade of the courtesan, the more one paid for her company. Among the most expensive were the qing guanren, the virgin courtesans. They were a kind of apprentice, to deflower whom was the privilege of only the very rich. Summoned to a party or an assignation, these girls made their way through the crush of Shanghai's alleys by riding on the shoulders of their ponces.

Whatever her rank, it was the dream of every singsong girl—who knew only too well how transient were her bloom and beauty—to become the principal wife of her patron. Sadly, the dream seldom came true, for while a man was happy enough to take his favourite singsong girl as a concubine, he demurred at making her his wife.

Shanghai's History through its Names

When the Chinese want to be literary, or brief, they call Shanghai 'Hu'. The name bespeaks Shanghai's origins as a fishing village, for *hu* is a bamboo fishing device, used in the third century by the people who lived around the Songjiang River (which was subsequently renamed Wusong River, and which forms the upper reaches of the Suzhou Creek). Shanghai is also sometimes known as Chunshen—or Shen for short—because in the third century BC, at the time of the Warring States (475–221 BC), the site on which the city now stands was a fief of the Lord Chunshen, prime minister to the King of the State of Chu. Another name with which Shanghai is associated is Huating. This was a county established in 751, over an area which covers part of present-day Shanghai.

Shanghai took its name from the Shanghai River, a tributary, long since gone, of the Songjiang. A township sprang into being on the west bank of the river, as, recognising its natural advantages as a port, junks and ships came to berth there. This was Shanghai, which presently became the largest town in Huating County. In 1292, Shanghai and four other towns in Huating were brought together to form the County of Shanghai. It was at about this time that the Songjiang was renamed the Wusong River.

But today when most Chinese think of Shanghai, they think not so much of the Wusong as of the Huangpu River. Shanghai's qualifications as a deep water port were greatly improved when a canal—forming that part of the Huangpu downstream of Waibaidu Bridge—was dredged and widened in the fourteenth century. Ships crowded the wharves of Shanghai, and the port itself grew in size and importance, thriving off the trade in cotton and other goods between the coast and the inland provinces on the Yangzi (Yangtse) River.

These were the foundations upon which the Western powers built when, with the opening of Shanghai as a Treaty Port, they came and carved out their enclaves there. The first of the foreign settlements, the British Concession, was bounded on the east along the Huangpu River by the Bund (today's Zhongshan Dong Yi Lu), on the west by Yu Ya Ching Road (today's Xizang Zhonglu), and on the south by the Yangjingbang Creek (which, after it was filled, was named Avenue Edward VII and which is now called Yan'an Donglu). The creek separated the British from the French Concession; the latter started from a wedge between the British Concession and the old Chinese city, and then ballooned out to a large area to the southwest of the city. To the north of the Suzhou Creek, in the district known then and now as Hongkou, lay the American Concession. This was later merged with the British Concession to form the International Settlement.

In the British Concession, the streets spread out behind the Bund in a grid. The main thoroughfare, Nanking Road (Nanjing Lu), ran eastwards from the Bund. The streets parallel to it were named after China's other cities (such as Canton, Fuzhou and Ningbo), while those which ran perpendicular to it (i.e north-south) were named after the provinces (such as Henan, Sichuan and Zhejiang). There was no mistaking the French Concession, because most of the streets there had French names: Rue Lafayette, Avenue Foch, to name but two. The smartest was Avenue Joffre (today's Huaihai Lu), which was to the French Concession what Nanking Road was to the British. Needless to say, these were all renamed when the communists took over.

THE CUSTOM HOUSE, SHANGHAI.

The Custom House, Shanghai

Excursions from Shanghai

SUZHOU AND HANGZHOU

'In heaven there is paradise; on earth there are Suzhou and Hangzhou' is a proverb known to every Chinese. While today both of these earthly paradises have been invaded to some extent by industries and modern buildings, they still have considerable charm.

■ SUZHOU

Suzhou is the nearer of the two (2 hours by car, 90 minutes by train) and makes a pleasant day trip. Known as the Venice of the East, the old part of town is still a city of canals, hump-backed bridges, and low, white-washed houses. Above all, Suzhou is famous for its exquisite gardens, over 100 of which survive. The **Garden of the Master of the Fishing Nets** (part of which has been reproduced in the Metropolitan Museum in New York), the **Humble Administrator's Garden** and the **Lingering Garden** are some fine examples. The city is also notable for its silk production, silk embroidery and other handicrafts such as sandalwood fans.

Dancers practise their tango, one of many early morning activities on Shanghai's Bund

■ HANGZHOU

Hangzhou's fabled **West Lake** is probably China's best-known beauty spot. With its willow trees, lotus blossoms in July and arched stone bridges, it conforms to everyone's idea of what Chinese scenery should look like. Many Chinese come here for their honeymoon. The huge lake has four landscaped islands and the whole area is dotted with pavilions and temples.

In addition to enjoying the scenery, you may visit silk factories (as in Suzhou) and also one of the tea plantations producing the famous Hangzhou Longjing (Dragon Well) tea.

Hangzhou is three to four hours by train from Shanghai or 30 minutes by plane. It can be visited in a day, but an overnight stay is recommended to relax and enjoy the atmosphere.

SHANGHAI'S OUTLYING COUNTIES

Those with more time who have seen Shanghai's major sights and visited Suzhou and Hangzhou might be interested in visiting some of the outlying counties, which are part of Shanghai Municipality.

■ SONGJIANG COUNTY

In Songjiang, a county seat for over 2,500 years and situated 19 kilometres (12 miles) southwest of Shanghai, is the beautiful **Square Pagoda**, which is 900 years old. Although renovated in 1975, much of the 11th-century brick and wood structure is original. It is over 48 metres (157 feet) high with nine storeys and was once part of Xingshengjiao Temple, of which one hall remains. There is also a Tang-dynasty stele, engraved with Buddhist scriptures, lions' heads, lotus petals and cloud patterns. It is said that the stele was erected to redeem the souls of criminals who were executed here.

A lovely example of a classical Chinese garden, with bizarre rocks, ponds and miniature landscaping, can be seen on a visit to **Zhuibaichi Park**. This once private garden probably dates from the late Ming dynasty and became the villa of a painter, Gu Dashen, in the mid-17th century.

The local speciality is Four-grilled Perch, which is rather rare and has been known for centuries as 'the number one dish south of the Yangzi'. Emperor Yang of the Sui dynasty praised the fish, saying it was 'as precious as gold and jade', while the Qing emperor Qianlong (reigned 1736–96) had it sent to him annually.

■ JIADING COUNTY

Twenty-five kilometres (15.5 miles) northwest of Shanghai is Jiading County, where a **Confucian temple** has existed since the 13th century. In the courtyard, stelae set into plinths of stone turtles record the temple restorations and meritorious deeds of various officials. Three old cypress trees are all that are left of 60 planted in the Yuan dynasty (1279–1368). Memorial tablets of Confucius' disciples and records of the achievements of local scholars line two corridors, which are part of the county museum.

Five streams converge at the site of the **Huilong Tan (Pool of Convergent Dragons)**, and adorning the surrounding stone railings are 72 different lions (Confucius had 72 disciples). During the Taiping Rebellion, the soldiers of the Dagger Society were bound to the trees beside the pool and executed. **Yingkui Hill** in the centre of the pool dates from the Ming dynasty, while the **Literary God Tower**, on the eastern bank, was restored recently after being bombed in the Sino-Japanese War.

The **Garden of Autumn Clouds (Qiuxia Pu)**, near Huilong Pool, is another example of private garden architecture. This was laid out by Minister of Defence, Gong Hong, in around 1520. Another garden, **Guyi Yuan (Garden of Ancient Splendour)**, built by a high official of the Ming dynasty, can be seen at the town of **Nanxiang** in Jiading County.

Nanxiang dumplings are famous in the area, their skin being especially thin. Chen He set up his dumpling shop 100 years ago and his recipe was so successful that the dumplings took on the name of the town, rather than of his shop.

■ QINGPU COUNTY
Qingpu county is 22.5 (14 miles) west of Shanghai. It is Shanghai's main supplier of freshwater fish.

DIANSHAN LAKE
This huge lake covers 6,300 hectares (15,570 acres), some 12 times larger than Hangzhou's West Lake, and teems with fish, freshwater shrimp and crabs. A holiday resort popular with Shanghainese has been developed near Yangshe Village on the southeastern stretch of the lake.

DAYING LAKE
The **Garden of Meandering Stream (Qushui Yuan)**, on the banks of the lake, is also a popular excursion for Shanghainese. It was built with funds donated by local townsfolk in 1745 and redeveloped in 1927.

Practical Information

As most travellers on the Yangzi will be sleeping on board ship, this section contains a selection of hotels, useful addresses and information on food and shopping in the major cites only.

Travel Agents

The following are a selection of the many companies which arrange Yangzi Cruises, listed in alphabetical order.

■ ABERCROMBIE AND KENT INTERNATIONAL, INC.
USA:
  1520 Kensington Road
  Oak Brook, Il 60521
  Tel (708) 954-2944, toll free (800) 323-7308, tlx 210126, fax (708) 954-3324

HONG KONG:
  19th Floor, Gitic Centre
  28 Queen's Road East
  Wanchai, Hong Kong
  Tel 2865-7818, tlx 78090, fax 2866-0556

Abercrombie and Kent International has been arranging deluxe cruises on the Yangzi River for many years. Since 1995 they have been using Orient Royal Cruiser ships (see page 172).

■ CHINA TRAVEL SERVICE (CTS)
USA:
  2/F 212 Sutter Street
  San Francisco, CA 94108
  Tel (415) 398-6627, toll-free (800) 332-2831, tlx 278233, fax (415) 398-6669

(LOS ANGELES)
  223 E. Garvey Ave., Suite 138
  Monterey Park, CA 91754
  Tel (818) 288-8222, tlx 372-3908, fax (818) 288-3464

*Qingpu County, with its canals and whitewashed cottages,
reflects the surrounding countryside of Jiangsu Province*

HONG KONG:
   (Main Office)
   4/F CTS House, 78–83, Connaught Road Central
   Tel 2853-3533, tlx 85222, fax 2541-9777

CTS's week-long tour begins and ends in Hong Kong. CTS Hong Kong's subsidiary, China Travel Air Service, is in the same office and runs charter flights to Chong-qing.

■ ORIENT ROYAL CRUISER LTD
CHINA:
   (Head Office)
   Wuhan No.14 pier
   Yangjiang Road
   Hankou
   Wuhan 430021
   Tel (027) 582-4686, fax (027) 582-3795

HONG KONG:
   1816–1817 Sun Hung Kai Centre
   30 Harbour Road
   Wanchai
   Hong Kong
   Tel 2824-9022, fax 2824-9092

While the *East Queen* and *East King* were built in China in 1994, most of the equipment and materials were imported from overseas in order to meet the highest international standards of marine technology.

■ REGAL CHINA CRUISES
CHINA:
   (Head Office)
   645 North Zhongshan Road
   Nanjing 210011, Jiangsu Province
   Tel (025) 881-6886, fax (025) 881-6880

USA:
   57 West 38th Street
   New York, New York
   Tel toll free (800) 808-3388, (212) 768-3388, fax (212) 768-4939

The new German-built *Princess Elaine*, *Princess Jeannie* and *Princess Sheena*, operated by Regal China Cruises are presently some of the most deluxe ships on the river. Many foreign tour operators include a cruise on one of these boats as part of their tours.

■ VICTORIA CRUISES INC.
USA:
    57–08 39th Ave.
    Woodside NY 11377
    Tel (212) 818-1698, fax (212) 818-9889

Victoria Cruises manage six deluxe ships (*MS Victoria I* to *VI*) built in 1994 for the Chongqing Shipping Company. Like Regal Cruises, they offer a choice of trips from four to ten days, and their cruises are featured by many foreign tour operators.

■ VOYAGES JULES VERNE
ENGLAND:
    21 Dorset Square
    London, NW1 6QG
Tel (171) 616-1000

Chongqing

■ HOTELS IN CHONGQING
Holiday Inn Yangtze Chongqing
15 Nanping Bei Lu, Tel 280-3380, tlx 62220, fax 280-0884
扬子江假日酒店　南坪北路 15 号
Chongqing's only international hotel, located on the southern bank of the Yangzi, ten minutes' drive from the city centre. It has 383 guest-rooms; facilities include coffee shop, bars, a variety of restaurants, disco, outdoor pool, health club and a business centre. Worldwide reservation through Holiday Inn sales offices.

Chungking Hotel (Chongqing Fandian)
41–43 Xinhua Lu. Tel 384-9301, tlx 62193, fax 384-3085
重庆饭店　新华路41-43号
Managed by a Hong Kong company, this is a well-run hotel, conveniently located in the city centre. Facilities include a beauty salon, a coffee shop serving Western food, and, in a second building, a business centre and small offices for rent to foreign businessmen. Reservations can be made through the Hong Kong sales

office: Soredic Co., 3911 Hong Kong Plaza, 186–191 Connaught Rd West, Hong Kong; Tel 2559-1021, tlx 84248, fax 2559-0197.

Renmin Guesthouse
175 Renmin Lu. Tel 385-1421, tlx 62127, fax 385-2076
人民宾馆　人民路175号
The two older wings of this hotel abut the Chongqing People's Assembly Hall, a fake Temple of Heaven built in the style of the original in Beijing. The annexe to the rear is a recent addition. Service is less than alert. Dining rooms serve Sichuan food.

Chongqing Guesthouse
235 Minsheng Lu. Tel 384-5888, tlx 62122, fax 383-0643
重庆宾馆　民生路235号
Not to be confused with the Chungking Hotel. Medium-range hotel in the heart of the city; restaurant, shop, bar and other usual services.

Huixian Lou
186 Minzu Lu, Tel 384-5027
会仙楼　民族路186号
Budget hotel in the downtown area. Dormitory beds available, restaurant.

■ SICHUAN CUISINE
Sichuan food is one of the four principal styles of Chinese cooking (the others are Cantonese, Peking and Huaiyang). The cuisine is characterized by hot piquant dishes heavily laced with red chillies, ginger and other condiments. Favourite local dishes include 'mother-in-law' beancurd (*mapo doufu*), double-cooked pork, diced chicken with hot peppers, *dandan* noodles, sour and hot soup, deep-fried beef strips and camphor-smoked duck.

■ USEFUL ADDRESSES IN CHONGQING
China International Travel Service/China Travel Service (Chongqing Branch)/ Chongqing Overseas Tourist Corp.
Renmin Guesthouse, 175 Renmin Lu. Tel 385-1665/0458, fax 385-0095/0196
中国国际旅行社／中国旅行社　人民路175号

Chongqing Changjiang Tourism Co.
Chaotianmen. Tel 382 7108, ticket office 382-9592, fax 384-4984
重庆长江旅游公司　朝天门
Contact either of the above for arranging passage on tourist cruise ships and regular passenger boats.

Steep field cultivation by the upper Yangzi, a major cause of erosion and river silt

The village of Meirendao in the Three Gorges—its population is being relocated by the government due to the new dam project

Chongqing Yangzi Shipping Passenger Ticket Office
Chaotianmen. Tel (enquiries) 384-1001
重庆长江航客运站售票处　朝天门
Contact for booking regular passenger boats.

Civil Aviation Administration of China (CAAC) Ticket Office
190 Zhongshan San Lu, Shangqingsi. Tel enquiries 52970, reservations 52198
中国民航售票处　中山三路190号

Chongqing Railway Station
Caiyuanba. Ticket desk Tel 53927, enquiries Tel 52607
重庆火车站　菜元坝

Chongqing Kangfulai Passengers Transportation Co Ltd.
58 Jian Xin Bei Lu, Jiangbeiqu. Tel 785-6619, 785-6639
重庆康福来客运公司　建新北路58号
Contact them for buses to Dazu.

Chongqing Antiques and Curio Store
238 Minsheng Lu. Tel 384-4255
重庆市文物商店　民生路238号

Yichang

■ HOTELS IN YICHANG
Pinghu Hotel
87 Dong Shan Road Tel 447788, tlx 417288, fax 447667
平湖大酒店　东山路87号
Currently the best hotel in Yichang, built in 1989. It has 173 guest rooms, a coffee shop and Chinese restaurant, business centre, health club and beauty salon.

Three Gorges Hotel (Sanxia Binguan)
38 Yanjiang Dadao. Tel 221922, tlx 40253, fax 442025
三峡宾馆　沿江大道38号
One of the newest and best hotels in Yichang.

Taohualing Hotel
29 Yunji Lu. Tel 442244, fax 445701
桃花岭饭店　云集路29号
A garden-style hotel in the downtown area. In the grounds are three old houses of the Treaty Port days.

■ USEFUL ADDRESSES IN YICHANG

Yichang General Tourist Corporation/China International Travel Service/China Travel Service
27 Yunji Lu. Tel 442282, fax 447064
中国国际旅行社宜昌分社　云集路27号

Civil Aviation Administration of China (CAAC) Ticket Office
167 Yiling Dadao. Tel 222648
中国民航售票处　夷陵大道167号

Wuhan

■ HOTELS IN WUHAN

Holiday Inn Tian An
868 Jiefang Dadao, Wuhan. Tel (027) 586-7888, fax 584-5353
大酒店　解放大道868号
Facilities in this 400-room hotel include three Chinese restaurants, a coffee shop, disco and bar, business centre and fitness centre.

Wuhan Asia Hotel
300 Jiefang Dadao, Hankou. Tel 568777, 566245, fax 556786. Reservations can be made through Free True Ltd., Room 3204–7, 32/F, Metro Plaza Tower 2, 233 Hing Fong Road, Kwai Chung, Hong Kong. Tel 2428-2880, fax 2418-5688
武汉亚洲大酒店　解放大道300号
This new joint-venture hotel has 265 rooms. Facilities include ten restaurants and bars, a business centre, a fitness centre and outdoor swimming pool.

Yangtze Hotel
539 Jiefang Dadao, Hankou. Tel 562828, tlx 40204, fax 554110
长江大酒店　解放大道539号
Excellent Cantonese and local Hubei cuisine restaurant on the eighth floor.

Victory Hotel (Shengli Fandian)
11 Siwei Lu, Hankou. Tel 231241, 232983, fax 232604
胜利饭店　汉口四唯路11号
This hotel is one of several renovated, older establishments in the city.

Jianghan Hotel
245 Shengli Jie, Hankou. Tel 211599, 211600, tlx 40150, fax 214342
江汉饭店　汉口胜利路245号
An older hotel that recalls the foreign presence in Hankou in the late 19th century. Renovated, but retaining its old character.

Xuangong Hotel
57 Jianghan Yi Lu, Hankou. Tel 210364, cable 2543, fax 216942
璇宫饭店　汉口江汉一路57号

Hankou Hotel
541 Jiefang Dadao, Hankou. Tel 557842, tlx 40203, cable 0219
汉口饭店　汉口解放大道541号

Qingchuan Hotel
88 Ximachang Jie. Tel 446688, 441143, cable 8550, fax 564964
晴川饭店　洗马长街88号
Location pleasant but out of the way. However, some of the tourist cruise boats
moor right in front of the hotel.

■ USEFUL ADDRESSES IN WUHAN
China International Travel Service (CITS) Hubei
48 Jianghan Yi Lu, Hankou. Tel 221265, 235649, tlx 40211, cable 1954,
fax 211891, 211706
中国国际旅行社武汉分社　江汉一路48号

Changjiang Cruise Overseas Travel Corp
89 Yanjiang Dadao. Tel 514931, 516412, 514005, tlx 40132, cable 4830,
fax 511049
中国国际旅行社长江分社　沿江大道89号

Wuhan Harbour Passenger Transportation Station
Wharf 23, Yanjiang Dadao, Hankou. Tel 231161, ext.3900
武汉港客运总站　汉口沿江大道23码头
Civil Aviation Administration Company (CAAC) Booking Office
217 Liji Bei Lu, Hankou. Tel passenger service 357186, information
centre 356780
中国民航　武汉利济北路217号

Wuhan Antiques Store
333 Zhongshan Dadao, Tel 356538
武汉古文物店　汉口中山大道333号

Nanjing

■ HOTELS IN NANJING

Jinling Hotel
Xinjiekou Square. Tel 445-5888, tlx 34110, fax 470-3396
金陵饭店　新街口汉中路2号
This 37-storey hotel provides international-standard accommodation and services. It has Western and Chinese restaurants and a revolving Sky Palace with a panoramic view of the city.

Dingshan Guesthouse
90 Chaha'er Lu. Tel 880-1868, tlx 34103, fax 882-1729
丁山宾馆　察哈尔路90号
A complex of buildings set in spacious grounds, the Dingshan offers a range of accomodation from renovated first-class bedrooms to cheaper lodgings in two blocks of prefabricated buildings.

Holiday Inn Yihua Nanjing
259 Zhongshan Bei Lu. Tel 343-8716, fax 342-6676
南京饭店　中山北路

Shuangmenlou Guesthouse
185 Huju Bei Lu. Tel 880-3961/3, tlx 34118, fax 880-1421
双门楼宾馆　虎踞北路185号
Another sprawling complex which contains the former British Consulate building (now quite shabby). The main building of this hotel has been modernized.

Xuanwu Hotel
193 Zhongyang Lu. Tel 330-3888, tlx 34026, fax 663-9624
玄武饭店　中央路193号
A recently-built hotel with a good location on the west side of Xuanwu Lake Park.

■ NANJING (JIANGSU) CUISINE

Food in Nanjing's major hotels is usually of a high standard. Regional specialities include Nanjing pressed duck, mandarin fish stuffed with shrimp, and spare ribs in a rich soybean sauce. Cooking styles from other parts of China may also be sampled in Nanjing. The restaurants in the **Fuzi Miao (Confucius Temple)** area off Jiankang Lu south of the city centre, are worth trying for the Jiangsu fare.

■ SHOPPING IN NANJING

Zhongshan Lu and Xinjiekou are the main shopping boulevards of the city, and the People's Market (Renmin Shangchang) at 79 Zhongshan Nan Lu is the most centrally located department store. A vast emporium (Nanjing Shangchang) was recently opened in the north of the city; from this four-storeyed store you can get an inter- esting glimpse into the consumer side of contemporary Chinese life. From thermos flasks to refrigerators, its wares draw crowds of Nanjing's citizens as well as visitors from other provinces and the increasingly affluent townships in the Jiangsu countryside. Nanjing is also the source of Yunjin brocade—one of three main types made in China. Woven of fine gold and silver silk thread, it is decorative and ornate.

Friendship Store
No. 17 Hanzhong Lu. Tel 664-8974
友谊商店　汉中路17号

Foreign Languages Bookstore
165 Zhongyang Lu. Tel 330-2698
外文书店　中央路165号

Collected Treasures Antique Store (Jubaozhai)
9 Hanzhong Lu. Tel 774-2550
聚宝斋　汉中路9号

Jiangsu Antique Store
321 Zhongshandong Lu. Tel 664-4701
江苏文物商店　中山东路321号

Jinling Hotel (lobby shop and shopping arcade)
Xinjiekou Square.
金陵饭店小卖部　新街口
The hotel lobby shop sells imported spirits, chocolates, film, postcards. A separate shopping arcade houses a number of stores for handicrafts, souvenirs, English-language books, antiques and so on.

■ USEFUL ADDRESSES IN NANJING
China International Travel Service (CITS)
202–1 Zhongshan Bei Lu. Tel 334-6444, tlx 34024, fax 330-8954
中国国际旅行社　中山北路202-1号

Jiangsu Overseas Tourist Corp
255 Zhongshan Bei Lu. Tel 332-7672/8, Tlx 34119, fax 330-6002, 330-5568
江苏海外旅游局　中山北路 255 号

Civil Aviation Administration of China (CAAC) Booking Office
52 Ruijin Lu. Tel (Passenger) 664-3378
中国民航售票处　瑞金路 52 号

Zhenjiang

■ HOTELS IN ZHENJIANG
Jinshan Hotel
1 Jinshan Xi Lu. Tel 232970/1/6, tlx 360025
金山饭店　金山西路 1 号

Jingjiang Hotel
111 Jiefang Lu. Tel 222842–6
京江饭店　解放路 111 号

■ SHOPPING IN ZHENJIANG
Antique Store
191 Jiefang Lu.
友谊商店　解放路 105 号

Friendship Store
105 Jiefang Lu.
中国国际旅行社　健康路 25 号

■ USEFUL ADDRESSES IN ZHENJIANG
China International Travel Service (CITS)
25 Jiankang Lu. Tel 237538, 233287, tlx 360025, fax 236425
中国国际旅行社　健康路 25 号

Shanghai

■ HOTELS IN SHANGHAI
Some years ago, Shanghai had a notorious shortage of hotel rooms. But today the city has a glut of new hotels, many of which are designed to be of international

class. Management contracts have been negotiated with well-known hotel chains and higher standards have been achieved. The standard of service and maintainance in some of the Chinese-managed hotels can be erratic, however.

Below is a select list of some of the many hotels.

SUPERIOR

Holiday Inn Crowne Plaza Shanghai
400 Pan Yu Rd. (corner of Pan Yu and Xin Huan roads). Tel 6252-888; tlx 30310; fax 6252-8545
上海银星皇冠假日酒店　番禺路 388 号

Huating Sheraton
1200 Caoxi Bei Lu. Tel 6439-1000; tlx 33589; fax 6255-0830
华亭宾馆　漕溪北路 1200 号
Huge S-shape building with two exterior glass elevators. All the modern facilities one would expect, plus ten-pin bowling alley. The location is southwest of the city centre; there is a shuttle bus service.

Jinjiang Hotel
59 Maoming Lu. Tel 6253-4242; tlx 33380, fax 6472-5588
锦江饭店　茂名南路 59 号
In the heart of the old French concession, the Jinjiang was originally a private hotel for French residents of Shanghai. The hotel's oldest building, the north block, with its grand curving steps leading up to the columned entrance, dates from 1931. Several restaurants, a large shopping arcade, disco, fitness centre.

Portman Shanghai
1376 Nanjing Xi Lu. Tel 6279-8888; tlx 33272; fax 6279-8999
波特曼香格里拉酒店　南京西路 1376 号
Striking new hotel, part of the Shanghai Centre and flanked by office and residential apartment blocks that house the bulk of Shanghai's foreign businesses and expatriates. Comprehensive services, including theatre and lawn bowls. Management is by Shangri-la Hotels International.

Shanghai Garden
58 Maoming Lu. Tel 6415-1111, tlx 30159; fax 6415-8866
上海花园酒店　茂名南路 58 号
Built on the site of the former Cercle Sportif Francais (later the Jinjiang Club), this new high-rise hotel incorporates a part of the pre-1949 building in its ground and first floors. The magnificent oval ballroom, carefully restored to its former art deco grandeur, is worth a visit. Run by Japanese group Okura Hotels. All the usual sports and business facilities.

Shanghai Hilton International

250 Huashan Lu. Tel 6248-0000; tlx 33612; fax 6248-3848
上海静安希尔顿酒店　华山路 250 号
Conveniently located between the city's established commercial districts and the Hongqiao development zone. Full array of amenities—health centre, tennis and squash courts, swimming pool, business centre etc.

Shanghai JC Mandarin

1225 Nanjing Xi Lu. Tel 6279-1888; tlx 33939; fax 6279-1822
上海锦沧文华大酒店　南京西路 1225 号
Well-located hotel that stands opposite the Shanghai Centre. Efficient management by Singaporean group. Boasts all-weather swimming pool, fitness centre and other top-class services.

Westin Tai Ping Yang Hotel

5 Zunyi Nan Lu. Tel 6275-7576; tlx 33345; fax 6275-5420
上海威斯汀太平洋大饭店　遵义南路 5 号
Considered the top hotel in the Hongqiao development zone. Under Westin management. All modern amenities. It is 15 minutes by car from the hotel to the western end of Nanjing Xi Lu.

FIRST CLASS
Hotel Equatorial

65 Yanan Rd West. Tel 6248-1688; tlx 33345; fax 6248-1773
上海国际贵都大饭店　延安西路 65 号
A large hotel next door to the Hilton, with plenty of restaurants.

Jinjiang Tower

161 Changle Lu. Tel 6433-4488; tlx 33265; fax 6433 3265
新锦江大酒店　长乐路 161 号
Striking cylindrical tower, the flagship of Shanghai's Jinjiang Group, a business and property conglomerate. Set in the same complex as the older Jinjiang hotel buildings, the Tower has all the facilities of a top-class international hotel.

Ocean Hotel

1171 Dong Da Ming Rd. Tel 545-8888; tlx 30333; fax 545-8993
远洋宾馆　东大名路 1171 号
Located behind the wharfs of the northern banks of the river, this hotel, with its revolving restaurant, has spectacular views of the Bund and Pudong area.

Peace Hotel

20 Nanjing Dong Lu. Tel 6321-1244; tlx 33914; fax 6329-0300
和平饭店　南京东路 20 号

Built in the late 1920s and formerly known as the Cathay, this landmark with its distinctive green-roofed tower is probably the most famous hotel in Shanghai. Its annexe on the opposite side of the road was previously the Palace Hotel (1906). The Peace was renovated in 1990, but the revolving doors, art deco windows and ornate, heavily decorated eight-floor dining room have been retained and continue to echo the hotel's glamorous past.

Yangtze New World
2099 Yan'an Xi Lu. Tel 6275-0000; tlx 33675; fax 6275-0750
上海杨子江大酒店　延安西路 2099 号
Run by Hong Kong's New World Hotels International, this is a pleasant four-star hotel favoured by business visitors. Located on the airport road, next to the Westin. Amenities included gym, karaoke lounge and business centre.

STANDARD
Overseas Chinese Hotel (Huaqiao Fandian)
104 Nanjing Xi Lu. Tel 6327-6226; tlx 33909; fax 6372-3634
华桥饭店　南京西路 104 号
Built more than 60 years ago, this hotel with its Italian-style portico enjoys one of the best locations in Shanghai. Its rooms remain popular with overseas Chinese visitors.

Park Hotel
170 Nanjing Xi Lu. Tel 6327-5225; tlx 33932; fax 6327-6958
国际饭店　南京西路 170 号
This 1930s hotel is conveniently situated by Renmin park, close to the Overseas Chinese Hotel and similarly popular for its excellent location.

Shanghai Mansions
20 Bei Suzhou Lu. Tel 6324-6260; tlx 33007; fax 6306-5147
上海大厦　北苏州路 20 号
Another relic from the 1930s. Located on the north bank of the Suzhou Creek and overlooks the waterfront. This used to be Broadway Mansions, a smart residential hotel.

BUDGET
Pujiang Hotel
15 Huangpu Lu. Tel 6324-6388; fax 6324-3179
浦江饭店　黄浦路 15 号
Located across the street from Shanghai Mansions, overlooks the Huangpu River. It new houses the Shanghai Stock Exchange on the first floor.

Seagull Hotel
60 Huangpu Lu. Tel 6325-1599; tlx 33003; fax 6324-1263
海鸥饭店　黄浦路60号
Built as an appendage to the International Seamen's Club in 1985, this hotel is open to the general public.

■ SHANGHAI CUISINE
Shanghai cuisine is a variation of the Yangzhou style, which emphasizes presentation, fragrance and freshness. Full use is made of the products from this 'Land of Fish and Rice', such as prawns, crab, shad, mullet, duck, game, lotus seeds and roots. Yang-zhou cooking does not use much heavy seasoning, apart from soya sauce and sugar. Famous Shanghai dishes include 'drunken' chicken, 'lion's head' (pork meatballs with cabbage), smoked fish, mock goose, braised eel and shrimps fried with egg white.

As one might expect from such a city, almost every style of Chinese regional cuisine is available as well as a variety of European food. Shanghai freshwater crabs—in season from October to December—are so popular that they are flown to Chinese and Japanese gourmets overseas. In the old city bazaar (near the Yu Garden), all kinds of local snacks may be tried: sesame cakes, egg rolls, glutinous rice in lotus leaves, noodles, deep-fried dough sticks (*youtiao*), steamed bread and dumplings.

■ SHOPPING IN SHANGHAI
The Shanghai area is famous for many arts and crafts—papercutting, jade carving, Jiading straw weaving, ivory carving, lacquerware, and needlepoint (introduced at the turn of this century by Western missionaries). The tradition of Gu silk embroidery is over 300 years old. It began with a local official, Gu Mingshi, who was fond of giving silk embroideries, made by his concubines, as presents.

ANTIQUES, ARTS AND CRAFTS
Chuangxin Old Wares Shop
1297 Huaihai Lu.
创新古玩店　淮海路1297号

Guohua Porcelain Shop
550 Nanjing Dong Lu.
国华瓷器商店　南京东路550号

Shanghai Antique and Curio Store
218 Guangdong Lu.
上海文物商店　广东路218号

Shanghai Arts and Crafts Service Centre
190 Nanjing Xi Lu.
上海工艺美术品服务部　南京西路190号

Shanghai Arts and Crafts Trade Centre, Shanghai Exhibition Centre
1000 Yan'an Zhong Lu.
上海展览馆　延安中路1000号

Shanghai Changjiang Seal Carving Factory
722 Huaihai Zhong Lu.
上海长江刻字厂　淮海中路722号

DEPARTMENT STORES
Friendship Store
33 Beijing Dong Lu.
友谊商店　北京东路33号

Shanghai No. I Department Store
830 Nanjing Dong Lu.
上海第一百货公司　南京东路830号

Hualian Department Store
(previously the Shanghai No. 10 Department Store) 635 Nanjing Dong Lu.
华联商厦　南京东路635号

■ USEFUL ADDRESSES IN SHANGHAI
China International Travel Service (CITS)
33 Zhongshan Dong Yi Lu. Tel 321-7200, tlx 33277, fax 329-1788
中国国际旅行社　中山东一路33号

China Travel Service (CTS)
881 Yan'an Zhong Lu. Tel 247-8888, tlx 33301, fax 247-5521
中国旅行社　延安中路881号

China Eastern Airlines Booking Office
200 Yan'an Xi Lu. Tel 247-2255, 247-1960, tlx 30210, fax 247-6761
东方航空公司售票处　延安西路200号

Dragonair Hong Kong
Room 123, North Wing, Jinjiang Hotel, 59 Maoming Nan Lu. Tel 433-6435,
258-2582 ext.123, fax 433-4814
港龙航空公司　茂名南路59号

Chronology of Periods in Chinese History

Paleolithic	c.600,000–7000 BC
Neolithic	c.7000–1600 BC
Shang	c.1600–1027 BC
Western Zhou	1027–771 BC
Eastern Zhou	770–256 BC
Spring and Autumn Annals	770–476 BC
Warring States	475–221 BC
Qin	221–207 BC
Western (Former) Han	206 BC–AD 8
Xin	9–24
Eastern (Later) Han	25–220
Three Kingdoms	220–265
Western Jin	265–316
Northern and Southern Dynasties	317–581
Sixteen Kingdoms	317–439
Former Zhao	304–329
Former Qin	351–383
Later Qin	384–417
Northern Wei	386–534
Weste	535–556
Northern Zhou	557–581
Sui	581–618
Tang	618–907
Five Dynasties	907–960
Liao	916–1125
Northern Song	960–1127
Southern Song	1127–1279
Jin (Jurchen)	1115–1234
Yuan (Mongol)	1279–1368
Ming	1368–1644
Qing (Manchu)	1644–1911
Republic of China	1911–1949
People's Republic of China	1949–

A Guide to Pronouncing Chinese Names

The official system of romanization used in China, which the visitor will find on maps, road signs and city shopfronts, is known as *Pinyin*. It is now almost universally adopted by the western media.

Some visitors may initially encounter some difficulty in pronouncing romanized Chinese words. In fact many of the sounds correspond to the usual pronunciation of the letters in English. The exceptions are:

Initials
c   is like the *ts* in 'i*ts*'

q   is like the *ch* in '*cheese*'

x   has no English equivalent, and can best be described as a hissing consonant that lies somewhere between *sh* and *s*. The sound was rendered as *hs* under an earlier transcription system.

z   is like the *ds* in 'fa*ds*'

zh is unaspirated, and sounds like the *j* in 'jug'

a   sounds like '*ah*'

e   is pronounced as the *o* in 'm*o*ther'

i   is pronounced as in 'ski'(written as *yi* when not preceded by an initial consonant). However, in *ci, chi, ri, shi, zi* and *zhi*, the sound represented by the *i* final is quite different and is similar to the *ir* in 'sir', but without much stressing of the *r* sound.

o   sounds like the *aw* in 'law'

u   sounds like the *oo* in '*ooze*'

ü   is pronounced as the German *ü* (written an *yu* when not preceded by an initial consonant). The last two finals are usually written simply as *e* and *u*.

Finals in Combination
When two or more finals are combined, such as in *hao, jiao* and *liu*, each letter retains its sound value as indicated in the list above, but note the following:

ai is like the *ie* in 'tie'

ei is like the *ay* in 'bay'

ian is like the *ien* in 'Vienna'

ie   similar to *ye* in'yet'

ou   is like the *o* in 'code'

uai sounds like 'why'

uan is like the *uan* in 'iguana' (except when preceded by *j, q, x* and *y*; in these cases a *u* following any of these four consonants is in fact *ü* and *uan* is similar to *uen*).

ue   is like the *ue* in 'duet'

ui   sounds like 'way'

Examples

A few Chinese names are shown below with English phonetic spelling beside them:

Beijing	Bay-jing (*jing* sounds like *ging* in 'paging')
Cixi	Tsi-shee
Guilin	Gway-lin
Hangzhou	Hahng-jo
Kangxi	Kahng-shee
Qianlong	Chien-loong
Tiantai	Tien-tie
Xi'an	Shee-ahn

An apostrophe is used to separate syllables in certain compound-character words to preclude confusion. For example, *Changan* (which can be *chang-an* or *chan-gan*) is sometimes written as *Chang'an*.

Tones

A Chinese syllable consists of not only an initial and a final or finals, but also a tone or pitch of the voice when the words are spoken. In *Pinyin* the four basic tones are marked ‾ ′ ˇ ˋ. These marks are almost never shown in printed form except in language-learning texts.

Recommended Reading

General Background
A History of Chinese Civilization Jacques Gernet, translated by J R Forster (Cambridge Press, Cambridge 1982)

Yangtse: Nature, History and the River Lyman P Van Slyke (Addison-Wesley Publishing Company Inc., Reading, Massachusetts 1988)

Sail and Sweep in China G R G Worcester (British Science Museum, 1966). A detailed account of the types of boats which frequented the rivers of China.

In Search of Old Shanghai Pan Ling (Joint Publishing Company, Hong Kong 1982)

In Search of Old Nanjing Barry Till (Joint Publishing Company, Hong Kong, 1982)

Travel and Exploration Along the Yangzi
The River of Golden Sand: The Narrative of a Journey through China and Eastern Tibet to Burmah William Gill (John Murray, London 1880; Gregg International Publishers Ltd. Farnborough Hants, U.K., 1969)

The Land of the Dragon: My Boating and Shooting Excursions to the Gorges of the Upper Yangtse William Percival (Hurst & Blackett Ltd., 1889)

An Australian in China G E Morrison (London: Horace Cox 1895; Oxford University Press 1985)

Through the Yangtse Gorges Archibald Little (Sampson, Low, Marston & Co., London 1898; Ch'eng Wen Publishing Co., Taipei 1972)

A Yankee on the Yangtze William Edgar Geil (Eaton & Mains, Cincinnati, 1904)

The Yangtse and the Yak: Adventurous Trails in and out of Tibet Marion H Duncan (Edwards Brothers, Inc., Ann Arbor, Michigan 1952)

Sailing Through China Paul Theroux (Houghton Mifflin Co., Boston, Massachusetts 1984)

Exploring the Yangtse, China's Longest River How Man Wong (Odyssey Productions Ltd., Hong Kong 1989)

To the Source of the Yangtse Dick Bell (Hodder & Stoughton, London 1991)

The River at the Centre of the World: A Journey Up the Yangtze and Back in Chinese Time Simon Winchester (Viking, London 1997). The author follows the river from the East China Sea to its source and paints a compelling and unforgettable picture in his 3,900 mile journey.

LITERATURE, AUTOBIOGRAPHY

Romance of the Three Kingdoms Luo Guangzhong (Charles E Tuttle Co. Inc., Tokyo 1973). The classic 14th-century novel about the three warring states along the Yangzi. In *Excerpts from Three Classical Novels* (Panda Books, Beijing, 1981), there is an excerpt from the novel, entitled *The Battle of the Red Cliff*, that vividly describes this event at a site just above Wuhan.

The Scholars Wu Ching-tzu (Translated by Yang Hsien-yi and Gladys Yang, Foreign Languages Press, Beijing 1973)

The Poetry and Career of Li Po Arthur Waley (George Allen & Unwin, 1989)

Li Po and Tu Fu Selected and Translated with an Introduction and Notes by Arthur Cooper (Penguin Books, Harmondsworth 1973)

100 Tang and Song Ci Poems Selected by Xu Xuanzhong (Commercial Press, Hong Kong 1986)

Destination Chungking Han Suyin (Jonathan Cape, London 1942; Panther Books, London 1973)

A Single Pebble John Hersey (Alfred A Knopf Inc., New York 1956; Vintage Books Edition, Random House Inc., New York 1989)

Yangzi River: The Wildest, Wickedest River on Earth An anthology selected and edited by Madeleine Lynn (Oxford University Press, Hong Kong 1997). This new collection of writing, spanning 13 centuries, offers a literary history of China's longest river, including classical poetry, Victorian memoirs and contemporary travel writing.

Index of Places

Practical information, such as telephone numbers and opening hours, is notoriously subject to change. We welcome corrections and suggestions from guidebook users; please write to:
The Guidebook Company, G/F 2 Lower Kai Yuen Lane, North Point, Hong Kong.
E-mail: odyssey@asiaonline.net